Interviewing of Suspects with Mental Health Conditions and Disorders in England and Wales

T0352726

Interviewing of Suspects with Mental Health Conditions and Disorders in England and Wales explores cutting-edge research that focuses specifically on these adults (including their cognitive needs and psychological vulnerabilities), the impact on the investigative interview, and existing legislation, guidance, and practice.

The book opens with a historical overview of the move from interrogation to investigative interviewing, including the impact of well-known miscarriages of justice and the inquiry that led to the development of current best practice interviewing. Further chapters focus on the concept of vulnerability within current theoretical frameworks, with a particular emphasis on mental health conditions and disorders, including how they are constructed, understood, and identified within legislation and by those working at the forefront of the criminal justice system. The book also examines current safeguards available to the suspect with mental health conditions and disorders, such as the Appropriate Adult; contemporary research explores their involvement with vulnerable suspects and whether it is sufficient, as well as how the Appropriate Adult understands and experiences their role. Final chapters scrutinise current best practice investigative interviewing of suspects with mental health conditions and disorders, and a paradigm shift towards an emerging evidence-based interview model that considers the vulnerabilities associated with suspects with mental health conditions and disorders in the investigative interview.

Examining current psychological theory, contemporary research, and existing legislation and guidance including authorised professional practice, this book will be of interest to those working within the criminal justice system, as well as policing and forensic psychology students. In particular, it is essential reading for all serving and trainee police officers, those delivering investigative interviewing training, and interviewing personnel, such as Appropriate Adults.

Dr Laura Farrugia is Senior Lecturer and Programme Leader in Forensic Psychology at the University of Sunderland and also works as a Registered Intermediary (accredited by the Ministry of Justice), assisting with vulnerable victims/witnesses at the police interview and trial stage. Her research looks at how individuals with mental health conditions and disorders are perceived within the criminal justice system and the role of Appropriate Adult during interviews with vulnerable suspects, as well as false confessions and miscarriages of justice. Her work focuses strongly on the investigative interviewing of vulnerable individuals. In addition, she examines the way in which police officers evaluate their own interviews. Dr Farrugia is one of the founding members of the Forensic Interview Trace.

Routledge Frontiers of Criminal Justice

The Virtual Reality of Imprisonment in Russia
"Preparing myself for Prison" in a Contested Human Rights
Landscape
Laura Piacentini and Elena Katz

Life Without Parole
Worse than Death?
*Ross Kleinstuber, Jeremiah Coldsmith, Margaret E. Leigey and
Sandra Joy*

Penal Responses to Serious Offending by Children
Principles, Practice and Global Perspectives
Nessa Lynch, Yannick van den Brink and Louise Forde

A Restorative Approach to Family Violence
Feminist Kin-Making
Joan Pennell

**Interviewing of Suspects with Mental Health Conditions and Disorders in
England and Wales**
A Paradigm Shift
Laura Farrugia

Convictions Without Truth
The Incompatibility of Science and Law
Robert Schehr

For more information about this series, please visit: www.routledge.
com/Routledge-Frontiers-of-Criminal-Justice/book-series/RFCJ

Interviewing of Suspects with Mental Health Conditions and Disorders in England and Wales

A Paradigm Shift

Laura Farrugia

Routledge
Taylor & Francis Group

LONDON AND NEW YORK

First published 2022
by Routledge
4 Park Square, Milton Park, Abingdon, Oxon OX14 4RN

and by Routledge
605 Third Avenue, New York, NY 10158

Routledge is an imprint of the Taylor & Francis Group, an informa business

© 2022 Dr Laura Farrugia

British Library Cataloguing-in-Publication Data
A catalogue record for this book is available from the British Library

Library of Congress Cataloging-in-Publication Data
A catalog record has been requested for this book

ISBN: 978-0-367-75110-4 (hbk)
ISBN: 978-0-367-75113-5 (pbk)
ISBN: 978-1-003-16102-8 (ebk)

DOI: 10.4324/9781003161028

Typeset in Times New Roman
by Newgen Publishing UK

"We must meet the challenge rather than wish it were not before us" (William Brennan).

For my boys.

Contents

List of Figures   x
List of Tables   xi

1   From Interrogation to Investigative Interviewing:
    A Historical Overview   1

2   The Concept of Vulnerability within the Criminal
    Justice System: What Does It Mean?   24

3   The Vulnerable Suspect and the Criminal Justice
    System: Identification, Safeguards, and Diversion   47

4   The Role of the Appropriate Adult: Passivity v
    Intervention   68

5   The Vulnerable Suspect: The Impact on the
    Investigative Interview   87

6   A Paradigm Shift: One Size Does *Not* Fit All?   110

7   New Directions: Implications and Future Research   129

    Index   148

Figures

1.1   The nine-step Reid Interrogation Technique   3
1.2   The PEACE model of interviewing   8
2.1   Police Experience Transitional Model   40
3.1   Graphical representation of the relationship between the
      type of case scenario and the disposal outcome   56
6.1   Accuracy of IRI in best practice and modified interview
      models   121
6.2   Clarifications of questions in best practice and modified
      interview models   122

Tables

1.1 Seven key principles of investigative interviewing 10
1.2 Definition of question types 13
1.3 PIP investigative levels 15
2.1 Emergent conceptual categories and subcategories
    within the Police Experience Transitional Model
    (PETM) 35
3.1 Risk assessment questions from the Authorised
    Professional Practice guidance 48
3.2 Observation levels from the Authorised Professional
    Practice guidance 49
3.3 Participation from police force areas 54
3.4 Association between police force area and
    disposal option 57
4.1 Appropriate, inappropriate, and missed interventions 72
4.2 Table of superordinate and subordinate themes 78
5.1 Table of overall characteristics of interview sample 99
6.1 Table of participants' self-reported mental health
    conditions and disorders 118

1 From Interrogation to Investigative Interviewing

A Historical Overview

Interrogation and the Reid Technique

The concept of 'interrogation' describes a heuristic approach to interviewing suspects using coercive and manipulative techniques; importantly, these techniques were designed in order to obtain a confession. Prior to the 1980s, police officers in England and Wales received little or no training in interviewing suspects, thus often employed interviewing methods that sought a confession (Walkley, 1987). This confession-seeking ethos was bolstered at the time by many influential training manuals that drew on inappropriate practices and consequently informed early police interrogation manuals in England and Wales (Farrugia & Milne, 2012). One of those practices is known as the Reid Interrogation Technique (Inbau et al., 2013). Originally developed in the 1970s, the authors advocate for the use of a two-stage approach during a criminal investigation; the Behaviour Analysis Interview (BAI) and the nine-step interrogation process (see Figure 1.1).

The Behaviour Analysis Interview

Advocates for the BAI describe this stage as a non-accusatory question and answer session (Inbau et al., 2013). Other scholars suggest that law enforcement officers conducting the BAI are instructed to differentiate between innocent, truthful suspects and suspects that are being deceptive (Masip & Herrero, 2013). This is conducted by exploring the suspects' version of events, any independent sources who may be able to corroborate the suspects' version of events, and any potential motive or opportunity to commit the crime. During the BAI, law enforcement officers utilise standard investigative questions and 'behaviour-provoking' questions designed to elicit behaviour symptoms of a suspects' innocence or guilt through verbal and non-verbal behavioural indicators

DOI: 10.4324/9781003161028-1

(Inbau et al., 2013). For example, Inbau and his colleagues believe that liars are more likely to cross their legs or shift about in their chair and are thought to be less helpful than truth-tellers (Inbau et al., 2013). Whilst it is often claimed that it is possible to accurately detect when an individual is lying on the basis of nonverbal behaviours (Inbau et al., 2013), numerous scientific studies have indicated that these are unreliable indicators of deception (Granhag et al., 2015). For example, early research suggested that the verbal and non-verbal measures endorsed by Inbau and his colleagues as indictors of deception or guilt are unreliable, and are actually exhibited by innocent suspects (Vrij, 2005; Vrij et al., 2006). Furthermore, the more police officers endorsed the view regarding cues to detecting deception, the worse they became at distinguishing between truth and lies (Mann et al., 2004), with research indicating that police officers are no more likely to be able to differentiate between lies and truth than chance level (Vrij et al., 2007). More recent scholars have suggested that should the verbal and non-verbal measures of detecting deception be used, then the likelihood of incorrect judgments and miscarriages of justice is increased (Synnott et al., 2015).

Once the BAI has been conducted and if the interrogator believes that the suspects' behaviour indicates guilt, then the suspect is subjected to the nine-step interrogation. Here the interrogator will employ a range of coercive and manipulative techniques, such as active persuasion, minimisation (often by offering a moral excuse), and maximisation of the seriousness of the offence in order to overcome objections, overcome denials, and gain a confession. Inbau et al. (2013) advocate for an immediate interrogation given that the suspect is "...most vulnerable to interrogation immediately following interview because of his concern that the investigator detected his deception" (p.169).

The Reid technique is considered the gold standard of law enforcement across the United States of America (Gudjonsson & Pearse, 2011). For example, interrogators advocate that the accusatory approach employed is a successful technique for gaining a confession. However, the technique has been heavily criticised throughout the academic literature (Meissner et al., 2014). The use of psychological tactics such as repetitive questioning and fabricating evidence against the suspect increases the possibility of false information (Meissner et al., 2014). The Reid technique creates an environment whereby it is psychologically and emotionally more appealing to confess in order to escape the interrogation (Kelly & Meissner, 2016). It is only when the suspect has provided a confession that the interrogation ends. This approach to interrogation has been viewed as a major contributory cause in a number of

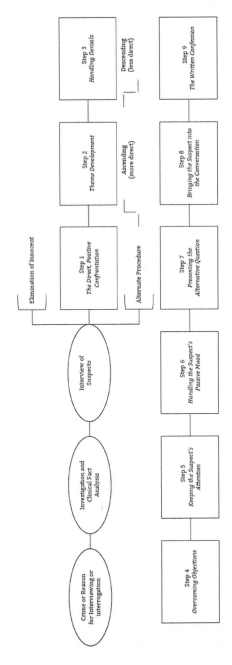

Figure 1.1 The nine-step Reid Interrogation Technique (Inbau et al., 2013)

miscarriages of justice involving a false confession (Gudjonsson, 2018; Kassin, 2005).

False Confessions and Miscarriages of Justice

It is hard to imagine that an innocent individual would knowingly confess to a crime that they did not commit, especially given the subsequent impact of a potential criminal conviction and custodial sentence. Unfortunately, false confessions and miscarriages of justice are not new phenomenon and are well documented within the academic literature (Drizin & Leo, 2004; Gudjonsson, 2018). Consequently, there is now a substantial literature base with organisations, such as the Innocence Project in the USA and the UK, reporting on wrongfully convicted individuals who have since been exonerated. Of note, approximately 30% of such cases involve a false confession as a contributing factor (Garrett, 2010).

What Is a False Confession?

Despite early insights from a Harvard psychology professor, Hugo Munsterberg (1908) in his book, *On the Witness Stand*, it was not until the 1980s that false confessions were widely discussed. The most central criterion in defining a false confession is that the individual confesses to a crime of which they are completely innocent (Gudjonsson, 2018). In their early work, Kassin and Wrightsman (1985) introduced a taxonomy that is now widely used when distinguishing between different types of false confessions. They highlight that there are three types:

(i)   Voluntary: Innocent individuals volunteer self-incriminating information without any coercion or pressure. There may be several reasons for doing so including protecting the actual perpetrator or a morbid desire for notoriety, particularly in high-profile cases.

(ii) Coerced-compliant: Innocent individuals confess to a crime due to the interrogative or coercive pressures experienced during the interrogation or interview, or because they believe that a confession may serve their own self-interest. Consequently, the individual is aware that the truth is different to what they are confessing; however, the individual may comply to the version of events being presented to them or for some immediate instrumental gain, for example, believing that they can go home and avoid further conflict (Gudjonsson, 2018). In these circumstances, there may be some awareness of the consequences of their confession, but the perceived immediate gains far outweigh the perceived long-term consequences.

(iii) Coerced-internalised: This occurs when the innocent individual comes to question their own innocence and comes to believe that they are responsible for the crime as a result of highly misleading claims about the evidence presented to them. In some cases, such individuals may come to confabulate memories to support their confession. Evidence suggests that this type of false confession is directly related to memory distrust – "a condition where people develop profound distrust of their memory recollections, as a result of which they are particularly susceptible to relying on external cues and suggestions" (Gudjonsson, 2003, p.196). Although memory distrust can be generated internally by the individual, it is often developed through prolonged and persuasive interviews or interrogations and may be particularly prevalent in individuals who are highly prone to fantasy or confabulation (Horselenberg et al., 2006).

Although other scholars have critiqued the Kassin and Wrightsman (1985) model of false confessions, it remains a useful framework and has since been extended and refined by others (Gudjonsson, 2003, Ofshe & Leo, 1997). It also provides some understanding as to the human decision-making involved in providing a false confession. Early research indicated that individuals will make decisions that they perceive to maximise their well-being given the constraints that they may face (Herrnstein et al., 1997) and that individuals are impulsive thus preferring immediate outcomes rather than delayed ones (Rachlin, 2000). Furthermore, in more recent experimental work, individuals tended to make admissions of misconduct to avoid the short-term consequence of denial even though it increased the risk of the larger long-term consequence (Madon et al., 2012). Thus, when short-sighted decision-making is used to characterise what suspects may face in an interrogation or interview, even suspects that refuse to confess at first will become exhausted over time and lose their will to resist (Davis & Leo, 2012). This has led to numerous miscarriages of justice around the world (Gudjonsson, 2018; Vrij et al., 2017).

The Fisher Inquiry and the Royal Commission

Perhaps one of the most influential miscarriages of justice relates to the murder of Maxwell Confait in the 1970s.

On 22nd April 1972, the body of Maxwell Confait was found in an upstairs bedroom in an address in southeast London. The home where Confait's body was found belonged to the landlord, Winston Goode, whom Confait had started renting a room from earlier that year. Two days later, a number of fires in the area led to the arrest of an 18-year-old male, Colin Lattimore, who admitted to lighting the fires with his friends, 15-year-old Ronnie Leighton and 14-year-old Ahmet Salih. All three males were arrested and interrogated without the presence of a parent or a guardian. During the interrogations, all three males admitted to starting the fire at the address where Confait was found, and Lattimore and Leighton also confessed to the murder to Confait. On 24th November 1972, Lattimore was found guilty of manslaughter on the grounds of diminished responsibility in addition to two counts of arson. Leighton was convicted for murder, arson, and burglary at a nearby address, and Salih was found guilty of burglary and arson. In 1974, the Court of Appeal quashed their convictions, labelling them as 'unsafe and unsatisfactory.' The case remains unsolved.

Although miscarriages of justice relating to coercive interview processes did not begin with the Maxwell Confait murder, it was in fact this case that pinpointed the contribution of the interview process to causing them in the UK (Price & Caplan, 1977). Upon quashing their convictions, the Court of Appeal identified that the confessions obtained had been gained from the males under improper police pressure (Williamson, 2007). This led to a public inquiry chaired by Sir Henry Fisher. His findings suggested that a flawed interview process coupled with the youths' psychological vulnerabilities led to them falsely confessing (Fisher, 1977). Such judicial concerns led to the Royal Commission on Criminal Procedure in England and Wales (RCCP, 1981). The judges' rules that previously governed police interviews prior to 1984 were found to be inadequate, and police were seen to be prioritising gaining a confession over searching for the truth by using oppressive questioning strategies or taking advantage of suspects' vulnerabilities (Irving, 1980). Consequently, it was this that paved the way for new legislation by advocating for a change in the current interviewing approach (Irving, 1980). The introduction of the Police and Criminal Evidence Act (PACE, 1984) and its associated Codes of Practice provided a legislative framework for the use of police powers, including arrest, investigation, and the interviewing of suspects. This ensured that interviews were audio-recorded and that all suspects were offered the right to free legal aid in an attempt to ensure fairness and transparency in the investigative process.

Investigative Interviewing and the PEACE Model

Despite the introduction of the PACE (1984), suspect interviewing remained poor. Although it was the official recognition of miscarriages of justice that helped drive the reforms, they were still occurring due to poor interviewing techniques. Thus, whilst PACE had increased the suspects' rights and introduced transparency to the investigative process, investigators were still driven by the same confession-seeking ethos (Baldwin, 1992). Consequently, there was still a need to move the questioning culture away from the previously used but ineffective coercive and manipulative techniques towards a more information-seeking style of interviewing. Amid such concerns over ineffective interviewing, in the early 1990s, the PEACE model of investigative interviewing (PEACE being a mnemonic for each stage of the model; Planning and preparation, Engage and explain, Account, clarify and challenge, Closure, and Evaluation), was developed and introduced to police officers in England and Wales (Williamson, 2006; see Figure 1.2).

Developed by extensive academic and practitioner collaborations, the PEACE model draws upon psychological research and recognises that information-gathering should play a core role in the planning of the investigative interview, as well as during the interview itself. Thus, police interview practices in England and Wales were encouraged to move away from interrogation and the coercive techniques previously used and shift to investigative interviewing, with an emphasis on obtaining accurate and reliable information. Training courses were introduced to each police service in England and Wales, and mandatory training was provided in relation to the PEACE model of interviewing. The five stages of the PEACE model are outlined below as per the guidance provided by the College of Policing (2020a).

Planning and Preparation

Described as one of the most important phases, the planning and preparation stage should consider all available information and identify key objectives for the purposes of the interview. Interviewers are directed to consider the use of an interview plan which should outline interview topics, points necessary to prove the potential offence or points that

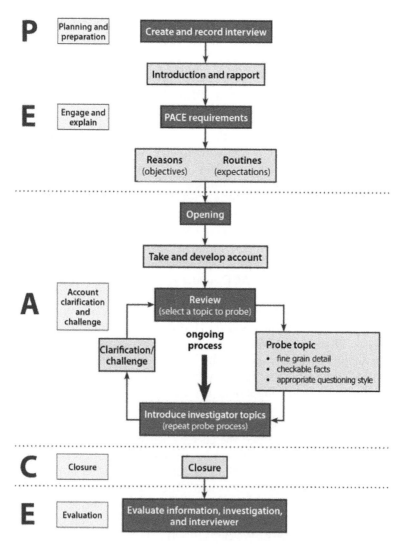

Figure 1.2 The PEACE model of interviewing (College of Policing, 2020a)

may be a defence, any exhibits, and preparation for a potential prepared statement, special warning, or significant comments or silences. Interviewers are also asked to consider interviewee characteristics including but not limited to age, gender, cultural background, domestic circumstances, and disability. Practical arrangements in order to assist the interviewee in understanding the circumstances of the offence should also be considered.

Engage and Explain

At this stage, interviewers are encouraged to try and engage with the interviewee by demonstrating active listening and building rapport (see Gabbert et al., 2020 for a full discussion). Clear reasons for the interview and the interview objectives should be explained at the start of the interview and interviewees should be informed that the interview is an opportunity to explain their involvement (or non-involvement) and encouraged to tell the interviewer anything that they believe is relevant.

Account, Clarify, and Challenge

Interviewers are encouraged to obtain as much information as possible during this stage. The use of appropriate questioning techniques, such as open-ended questions to elicit a free recall, should be used. In addition, demonstrating non-verbal behaviours, for example, appropriate posture, active listening, and prompting the interviewee to report their account until it is complete, is encouraged. Following the free recall, interviewers are directed to clarify and explore the interviewee's account by breaking it down into smaller, more manageable topics and systematically probing each topic until the account is fully explored. The interviewee's account may be challenged by information identified during the planning phase. Interviewers can employ one of two styles of interviewing in order to obtain as much information as possible: (i) the Conversation Management Approach (Shepherd, 2007) or (ii) the Cognitive Interview (Fisher et al., 1987).

Closure

Following the obtaining of a full account, the interviewer is encouraged to accurately summarise the interviewee's account as well as deal with any questions that may arise. The interviewer is then directed to formally end the interview and turn the recording off. Next steps in the investigation should be explained to the interviewee.

Evaluation

After the conclusion of an interview, the interviewer is encouraged to reflect upon and evaluate what information has been obtained with a

Table 1.1 Seven key principles of investigative interviewing

Principle	Description
Principle 1	The aim of investigative interviewing is to obtain accurate and reliable accounts from victims, witnesses, or suspects about matters under police investigation.
Principle 2	Investigators must act fairly when questioning victims, witnesses, or suspects. They must ensure that they comply with all the provisions and duties under the Equality Act 2010 and the Human Rights Act 1998.
Principle 3	Investigative interviewing should be approached with an investigative mindset.
Principle 4	Investigators are free to ask a wide range of questions in an interview in order to obtain material which may assist an investigation and provide sufficient evidence or information.
Principle 5	Investigators should recognise the positive impact of an early admission in the context of the criminal justice system.
Principle 6	Investigators are not bound to accept the first answer given. Questioning is not unfair merely because it is persistent.
Principle 7	Even when a suspect exercises the right to silence, investigators have a responsibility to put questions to them.

Source: College of Policing (2021).

view to determining whether any further action is necessary. How the account obtained fits with the rest of the investigation should also be reflected upon as should their own interviewer performance and adherence to current policy and practice.

In addition to the introduction of the PEACE model of interviewing, seven key principles were developed by the national strategic steering group to help increase the application of good investigative interviewing techniques and to assist interviewers on how to use the PEACE model framework (see Table 1.1).

Does PEACE Work?

The introduction of the PEACE model of interviewing and the core principles was designed to ensure that all police officers were provided with the necessary skills and training to conduct effective, information-seeking investigative interviews. One of the largest national evaluations of the PEACE model of interviewing conducted in 2001 found significant improvements in the quality of suspect interviews. Clarke and Milne (2001) analysed 177 taped suspect interviews and found that the overall interviewing style had improved, including the use of open-ended questions, the use of good communication skills, a reduction in leading questions, and little to no interruption of the suspects' account. However, the authors also reported that the listening skills of the interviewing officers remained poor and 10% of the interviews analysed contained possible breaches of PACE. Concerns were also raised regarding the effective planning and preparation for the interview as well as rapport building. Furthermore, weaknesses were found in procedural aspects such as the explanation of the caution and the purpose of the interview, and the closure stage. Other research conducted since has reported a similar mixed picture. Ethical interviewing techniques emphasised by the PEACE model have been commonly found in police interviews (Soukara et al., 2009; Walsh & Bull, 2010; Walsh & Milne, 2008). However, research conducted around a similar time indicated that poor practices still existed such as police officers reverting back to old interview techniques and using a high level of inappropriate questioning strategies (Griffiths & Milne, 2006; Oxburgh et al., 2010a; Oxburgh et al., 2010b; Wright & Powell, 2006). As such, early research into the effectiveness of the PEACE model appeared mixed.

Since the introduction of the PEACE model of interviewing, psychologists have systematically assessed its efficacy and developed an understanding of best practices based on scientific knowledge. Consequently, there now exists syntheses of literature exploring a variety of issues, which has subsequently led to the development of several protocols. For example, in the witness interviewing domain, protocols have been developed for child and adult witness interviewing (see, e.g., Benia et al., 2015, for a discussion of the National Institute of Child Health and Human Development (NICHD) protocol for child interviews), and science now exists that explores the detrimental impact of misinformation, stress/arousal, or alcohol on a witnesses' ability to recall information (Fawcett et al., 2013; Jores et al., 2019). Within suspect interviewing, the ability to detect deception (Bond Jr. & DePaulo, 2006; Hartwig & Bond Jr., 2011), and the efficacy of suspect interrogation approaches, has been explored, in addition to the prevalence of false confessions (Meissner et al., 2014; Stewart et al., 2018), and various psychological processes that occur within vulnerable and non-vulnerable suspect interviews. Such meta-analyses and systematic reviews are critical for evaluating the effectiveness of various investigative interviewing approaches in order to identify and develop evidence-based practices that investigators may then adopt. It is this availability of a large and growing body of scientific knowledge establishing that rapport-based, non-coercive methods for interviewing are the most effective for obtaining accurate and reliable information that led to the development of a set of international standards for investigative interviews (see Mendez, 2021, for a full discussion regarding 'Principles on Effective Interviewing for Investigation and Information Gathering').

The interviewing of suspects has come a long way from early interrogation techniques to the investigative mindset now employed by investigators in England and Wales and around the world. However, the drive to seeking information rather than a confession is dependent upon appropriate questioning strategies. Information obtained during the investigative interview can be crucial in furthering the investigation and any criminal proceedings.

Questioning Strategies in Investigative Interviews

The use of appropriate questioning methods is essential in ensuring not only that accurate and reliable information is gained but also that the interviewee recall or memory is not contaminated, and they are not led into agreeing to information that is incorrect. The police interviewing of a suspect is a particularly complex and interactive process (Haworth, 2013), and the importance of obtaining accurate and reliable information has been highlighted extensively (Fisher & Geiselman, 1992; Gabbert et al., 2016; Griffiths & Milne, 2006; Lamb et al., 2008; Oxburgh et al., 2010a; Shepherd, 2007). However, there remains some discrepancies between academics and practitioners in the classification of question types (Oxburgh et al., 2010a). In a review of the literature concerning question typology, Oxburgh and colleagues (2010a) reported that an open question is most commonly described as a 'TED' question – 'Tell,' 'Explain,' 'Describe' (e.g., Griffiths & Milne, 2006; Shepherd, 2007). However, it has also been defined as 'open-ended' (Davies et al., 2000), free report (Aldridge & Cameron, 1999), open-ended breadth and depth (Powell & Snow, 2007), invitational (Korkman et al., 2006) or a 5WH (What/Where/When/Why/Who/How; Centrex, 2004). This is also echoed when defining a probing question which is most commonly defined as a 5WH question but has also been identified as a closed identification question (Myklebust & Bjorklund, 2006), a directive question (Korkman et al., 2006) and a specific question (Milne & Bull, 1999). Closed questions – those that typically elicit a yes or no response, have also been defined as Yes/No questions (Myklebust & Bjorklund, 2006), specific questions (Aldridge & Cameron, 1999) and been split into appropriate closed (Griffiths & Milne, 2006) and inappropriate closed questions (Fiengo, 2007). Such inconsistencies are also reported in interview protocols. For example, Gabbert et al. (2016), in developing the Structured Interview Protocol, categorised questions as open prompts (breadth of information) – those that encourage a free recall, open prompts (depth of information) – those that seek further information but still utilise an open question, focused prompts (also known as the 5WH), and closed questions that include forced choice questions. Furthermore, the College of Policing identifies five key question types: (i) open-ended, defined as 'TED' questions, (ii) specific-closed, also known as the 5WH, (iii) forced-choice, those that provide interviewees with limited response options, (iv) multiple, a number of questions that are asked in one instance, and (v) leading, questions that either imply the answer or assume facts that are likely to be disputed (College of Policing, 2020b). Thus, there are varying definitions used by academic and practitioners alike when considering question typology. Table 1.2 provides an overview of the most commonly used question

Table 1.2 Definition of question types

	Question Type	Description
Appropriate Questions	Open	Questions that are open-ended and encourage a free recall; known as 'TED' questions, 'Tell,' 'Explain,' 'Describe'
	Probing	Questions that are designed to probe the account; known as the 5WH, 'What,' 'Where,' 'Who,' 'When,' 'Why'
	Encouragers/ Acknowledgements	Utterances that are designed to encourage the interviewee to continue talking, e.g., 'Uh huh'
Inappropriate Questions	Closed	Questions that are designed to elicit a 'yes' or 'no' response only
	Forced Choice	Questions that provide the interviewee with limited response options, e.g., 'Was the car red or white?'
	Leading	Questions that mention new pieces of information that have not been previously mentioned by the interviewee, typically quite leading in nature
	Opinion/Statements	An opinion or statement offered rather than a question being asked
	Multiple	A number of questions asked in one instance
	Echo	The interviewer repeats the response of the interviewee

types amalgamated from the literature base and used within the current textbook.

Despite the variance in classification systems of question types, the psychological literature repeatedly reports that open questions tend to elicit more detailed and more accurate information (Griffiths & Milne, 2006; Myklebust, 2009; Phillips et al., 2011; Snook et al., 2012). However, despite this plethora of research work, in practice, the reality remains that more inappropriate questions such as closed or leading questions are still commonly used during the police interview (Farrugia & Gabbert, 2019; Snook & Keating, 2011; Wright & Alison, 2004), despite police officers believing that they use more open and probing types of questions (Oxburgh et al., 2016) and despite police officers being trained in using appropriate questioning methods (Soukara et al., 2009).

The use of inappropriate questions is not conducive when conducting an investigative interview, particularly when the aim is to obtain accurate and reliable information. For example, the use of multiple questions can make it difficult for the suspect to understand which part they are meant to answer (Snook et al., 2012), whilst leading questions can lead to memory contamination, subsequently resulting in a decrease of accuracy and reliability of the information provided by the suspect (Bowles & Sharman, 2014). This is particularly hazardous if the interviewee is a vulnerable suspect. Furthermore, the use of closed questions that tend to elicit a 'yes' or 'no' response will often limit the amount of information gained. What can assist with maintaining appropriate questioning methods, however, is ongoing training and professionalisation.

Professionalising Criminal Investigation Programme and Authorised Professional Practice

Historically, criminal investigation and general policing were not viewed as too dissimilar to each other (Stelfox, 2009). The view that few skills were needed to conduct investigations was reinforced in the late 1970s and early 1980s (Burrows & Tarling, 1987). Consequently, the police service did not develop a standardised professional practice when investigating crimes until the early 2000s. In 2005, the Association of Chief Police Officers (ACPO) in England and Wales developed a national training and development programme which was designed "to enhance the crime investigation skills and ability of police officers and staff involved in the investigative process and to drive through new standards of investigation at all levels" (National Centre for Police Excellence [NCPE], 2005, p.1). In addition, the Professionalising Criminal Investigation Programme (PIP) was a key feature of the Government's police reform agenda (College of Policing, 2020b). Driven by the series of miscarriages of justice and subsequent Royal Commissions, it was designed to replace the five-tiered structure of interviewing skills that had previously been developed to provide police officers with theory-driven training specific to their career and other aspects of investigative interviewing (see Griffiths & Milne, 2006 for a full discussion of the five-tier interview strategy).

The creation of the PIP allowed for new standards to be embedded into investigative practice and introduced levels of qualification depending upon the type of investigations one would encounter. Underpinned by the Core Investigative Doctrine and procedural manuals including ACPO Murder Investigation Manual and the ACPO Investigative Interview Strategy, the aim was to signal an improvement in criminal investigation through training and development. The PIP introduced a training curriculum for investigators that now takes them from the basic levels of investigation through to the most complex and was subsequently adopted by ACPO as a national model for improving overall standards in criminal investigation. Focusing on four specific levels (see Table 1.3 for a description), the PIP now ensures that the professional practice of criminal investigation is supported by training and development.

In addition to the development of the PIP, Authorised Professional Practice (APP) was developed in 2012. Authorised and owned by the College of Policing as the official source of professional practice on policing, the aim is to equip officers with the skills and knowledge necessary to investigate crime (College of Policing, 2018). Covering all elements of policing, APP content includes guidance on (but not limited to) armed policing, covert policing, detention and custody, information management, investigation, and prosecution and case management, and police officers are expected to have regard to APP content when

Table 1.3 PIP investigative levels

Investigative Level	*Role and Description*
Level 1	Patrol constable, police staff, or supervisors investigating priority and volume crime
Level 2	Investigators including Detective Constables, Detective Sergeants, and Detective Inspectors as well as other specialist investigators involved in serious and complex crimes
Level 3	Senior investigating officers in management roles of major crimes
Level 4	Senior investigating officers in overall command of linked, series or major crimes

discharging their responsibilities. Furthermore, the College of Policing endorses the use of the 'National Decision Model' (NDM; College of Policing, 2014). Underpinned by six key elements, it is suitable for all decision-making within policing. The six key elements are:

(i)   Code of ethics: the principles that police members are expected to follow;
(ii)   Information: what information is known and what further intelligence is needed;
(iii) Assessment: assessment of the situation including any threats or risk;
(iv)   Powers and policy: consideration of police powers, policies, and legislation that could be applicable to the situation;
(v)   Options: consideration of options available in reaching a decision that is proportionate and reasonable to the circumstances;
(vi)   Action and review: implementation of decision and reflection on decision-making.

Thus, all police members are encouraged to follow this structured model to rationalise their decision making and subsequent actions during any incident, including the investigative interview.

Such professionalising of policing is also being propelled by the championing of Higher Education involvement in police training. A relatively new development, consideration is now given to police officers obtaining degrees in order to join the police and obtaining higher qualifications in order to progress with their career.

Summary

Miscarriages of justice destroy individuals' lives and erode public support for the criminal justice system. The role of the investigative process in causing injustice has been well documented through the many cases of false confessions. However, such miscarriages of justice can also serve as 'lessons to be learnt.' The contribution of psychological research over recent decades has proved invaluable in uncovering the impact of poor investigative practices on subsequent miscarriages of justice (Brants, 2008). As such, psychologists working with practitioners have helped to implement improvements to investigative processes in order to reduce further incidences of miscarriages of justice (Gudjonsson, 2018).

The introduction of the PACE (1984) and its associated Codes of Practice, the PEACE model of interviewing, and, more recently, the professionalisation of criminal investigation via the PIP and APP including the NDM have improved the accountability and operational decision-making and thus the overall quality of investigative work in England and Wales. Indeed, the materials produced by these combined initiatives serve as a standard toward which many other police services in other parts of the world aspire (Westera et al., 2016). The move from unethical, confession-seeking interrogation practices to information-seeking investigative interviewing has been one of the biggest changes to come about in investigative interviewing in many decades. Now aligned to the PIP process and APP content, police interviewing in England and Wales is unrecognisable from the questionable practices of the past.

Key Learning Points

- Prior to the 1980s, police officers in England and Wales received very little or no training in interviewing suspects subsequently employing tactics bolstered by police interrogation manuals such as the Reid technique.
- The Reid technique adopts the use of a BAI initially to identify if a suspect is being deceptive in their responses. If suspects are deemed to be so, the nine-step interrogation method is employed.
- Whilst the Reid technique is considered the gold standard of law enforcement across the USA, many scholars view this interrogation method as being a major contributory cause in a number of confession-fuelled miscarriages of justice.
- Kassin and Wrightsman (1985) taxonomy of false confessions identifies three main types: (i) voluntary, (ii) coerced-compliant, and (iii) coerced-internalised.
- The Maxwell Confait case triggered the Fisher Inquiry and subsequent RCCP in England and Wales in the early 1980s. This paved the way for the introduction of PACE (1984) and its associated Codes of Practice and the PEACE model of interviewing.
- Principles on effective interviewing have now been developed to ensure that international standards for investigative interviewing are met (Mendez, 2021).
- The importance of questioning during investigative interviews has been well documented. Despite the variance

in classification systems, there is a general consensus that open questions tend to elicit more detailed and more accurate information.

• Criminal investigation and police practices have now been professionalised since the introduction of the PIP and APP content from the College of Policing, including the NDM.

References

Aldridge, J. & Cameron, S. (1999). Interviewing child witnesses: Questioning techniques and the role of training. *Applied Developmental Science, 3,* 136–147.

Baldwin, J. (1992). *Video-taping police interviews with suspects – an evaluation.* London: Home Office.

Benia, L., Hauck-Filho, N., Dillenburg, M., & Stein, L. (2015). The NICHD investigative interview protocol: A meta-analytic review. *Journal of Child Sexual Abuse, 24*(3), 259–279.

Bond, C. Jr. & DePaulo, B. (2006). Accuracy of deception judgments. *Personality and Social Psychology Review, 10*(3), 214–234.

Bowles, P. & Sharman, S. (2014). A review of the impact of different types of leading interview questions on child and adult witnesses with intellectual disabilities. *Psychiatry, Psychology and Law, 21*(2), 205–217.

Brants, C. (2008). The vulnerability of Dutch criminal procedure to wrongful conviction. In R. Huff & M. Kilias (Eds.), *Wrongful conviction: International perspectives on miscarriages of justice* (pp. 157–181). Philadelphia: Temple University Press.

Burrows, J. & Tarling, R. (1987). The investigation of crime in England and Wales. *British Journal of Criminology, 27*(3), 229–251.

Centrex (2004). *Management of Volume Crime.* Harrogate: Centrex.

Clarke, C. & Milne, R. (2001). *National evaluation of the PEACE investigative interviewing course. Police Research Award Scheme, Report No. PRAS/149.* Portsmouth, UK: Institute of Criminal Justice Studies.

College of Policing. (2014). *National Decision Model.* www.app.college.police.uk/app-content/national-decision-model/the-national decision-model/

College of Policing. (2018). *Authorised Professional Practice.* www.app.college.police.uk/

College of Policing. (2020a). *Investigative Interviewing.* www.app.college.police.uk/app-content/investigations/investigative interviewing/

College of Policing. (2020b). *Professionalising Investigation Programme.* www.app.college.police.uk/app-content/investigations/introduction/

College of Policing. (2021). *Principles and ethics.* www.app.college.police.uk/app content/investigations/investigative-interviewing/#principles-and-ethics

Davies, G., Westcott, H., & Horan, N. (2000). The impact of questioning style on the content of investigative interviews with suspected child sexual abuse victims. *Psychology, Crime and Law, 6,* 81–97.

Davis, D. & Leo, R. (2012). Interrogation-related regulatory decline: Ego depletion, failures of self-regulation, and the decision to confess. *Psychology, Public Policy, and Law, 18*(4), 673–704.

Drizin, S. & Leo, R. (2004). The problem of false confessions in the post-DNA world. *North Carolina Law Review, 82,* 891–1007.

Farrugia, L. & Gabbert, F. (2019). Vulnerable suspects in police interviews: Exploring current practice in England and Wales. *Journal of Investigative Psychology and Offender Profiling, 17*(1), 17–30.

Farrugia, L. & Milne, R. (2012). Suspect interviewing and mental health in the UK: An overview. *Investigative Interviewing: Research and Practice, 4*(2), 25–42.

Fawcett, J., Russell, E., Peace, K., & Christie, J. (2013). Of guns and geese: A meta-analytic review of the 'weapon focus' literature. *Psychology, Crime & Law, 19*(1), 35–66.

Fiengo, R. (2007). *Asking questions: Using meaningful structures to imply ignorance.* Oxford: Oxford University Press.

Fisher, H. (1977). *Report of an inquiry by the Hon. Sir Henry Fisher into the circumstances leading to the trial of three persons on charges arising out of the death of Maxwell Confait and the fire at 27 Doggett Road, London, SE6.* London: HMSO.

Fisher, R. & Geiselman, R. (1992). *Memory-enhancing techniques for investigative interviewing: The cognitive interview.* Springfield, IL: Charles C. Thomas.

Fisher, R., Geiselman, R., & Raymond, D. (1987). Critical analysis of police interview techniques. *Journal of Police Science and Administration, 3,* 177–185.

Gabbert, F., Hope, L., La Rooy, D., McGregor, A., Ellis, T., & Milne, R. (2016). *Introducing a PEACE-compliant 'Structured Interview Protocol' to enhance the quality of investigative interviews.* Paper presented at the 9th annual conference of the International Investigative Interviewing Research Group (iIIRG), London, UK.

Gabbert, F., Hope, L., Luther, K., Wright, G., Ng, M., & Oxburgh, G. (2020). Exploring the use of rapport in professional information-gathering contexts by systematically mapping the evidence base. *Applied Cognitive Psychology, 35*(2), 329–341.

Garrett, B. (2010). The substance of false confessions. *Stanford Law Review, 62,* 1051–1119.

Granhag, P., Vrij, A., & Verschuere, B. (2015). *Detecting deception: Current challenges and cognitive approaches.* London: Wiley-Blackwell.

Griffiths, A. & Milne, R. (2006). Will it all end in tiers? Police interviews with suspects in Britain. In T. Williamson (Ed.), *Investigative interviewing: Rights, research, regulation* (pp. 167–189). Cullompton: Willan.

Gudjonsson, G. (2003). *The psychology of interrogations and confessions. A handbook.* Chichester: Wiley.

Gudjonsson, G. (2018). *The psychology of false confessions: Forty years of science and practice.* West Sussex: Wiley.

Gudjonsson, G. & Pearse, J. (2011). Suspect interviews and false confessions. *Current Directions in Psychological Science, 20*(1), 33–37.

Hartwig, M. & Bond, C. Jr. (2011). Why do lie-catchers fail? A lens model meta-analysis of human lie judgments. *Psychological Bulletin, 137*(4), 643–659.

Haworth, K. (2013). Language of police interviews. In C. Chapelle (Ed.), *The encyclopedia of applied linguistics* (pp. 1–5). Blackwell.

Herrnstein, R., Rachlin, H., & Laibson, D. (1997). *The matching law. Papers in psychology and economics.* Cambridge: Harvard University Press.

Home Office. (1981). *Royal Commission on Criminal Procedure.* London: HMSO.

Home Office. (1984). *Police and Criminal Evidence Act.* London: Home Office.

Horselenberg, R., Merckelbach, H., Sweets, T., Franssens, D., Peters, G., & Zeles, G. (2006). False confessions in the lab: Do plausibility and consequences matter? *Psychology, Crime and Law, 12*, 61–75.

Inbau, F., Reid, J., Buckley, J., & Jayne, B. (2013). *Criminal interrogation and confessions.* Burlington: Jones & Bartlett Learning.

Irving, B. (1980). *Police interrogation: A case study of current practice.* Royal Commission on Criminal Procedure, Research Study No. 2. London: HMSO.

Jores, T., Colloff, M., Kloft, L., Smailes, H., & Flowe, H. (2019). A meta-analysis of the effects of acute alcohol intoxication on witness recall. *Applied Cognitive Psychology, 33*(3), 334–343.

Kassin, S. (2005). On the psychology of confessions: Does innocence put innocents at risk? *American Psychologist, 60*, 215–228.

Kassin, S. & Wrightsman, L. (1985). Confession evidence. In S. Kassin & L. Wrightsman (Eds.), *The psychology of evidence and trial procedure* (pp. 67–94). London: Sage.

Kelly, C. & Meissner, C. (2016). Interrogation and investigative interviewing in the United States: Research and practice. In D. Walsh, G. Oxburgh, A. Redlich, & T. Myklebust (Eds.), *International developments and practices in investigative interviewing and interrogation: Volume 2: Suspects* (pp. 255–266). Abingdon: Routledge.

Korkman, J., Santtila, P., & Sandnabba, N. (2006). Dynamics of verbal interaction between interviewer and child in interviews with alleged victims of child sexual abuse. *Scandinavian Journal of Psychology, 47*, 109–119.

Lamb, M., Hershkowitz, I., Orbach, Y., & Esplin, P. (2008). *Tell me what happened: Structured investigative interviews of young victims and witnesses.* Chichester and Hoboken, NJ: Wiley.

Madon, S., Guyll, M., Scherr, K., Greathouse, S., & Wells, G. (2012). Temporal discounting: The differential effect of proximal and distal consequences on confession decisions. *Law and Human Behaviour, 36*(1), 13–20.

Mann, S., Vrij, A., & Bull, R. (2004). Detecting true lies: Police officers' ability to detect deceit. *Journal of Applied Psychology, 89*, 137–149.

Masip, J. & Herrero, C. (2013). What would you say if you were guilty? Suspects strategies during a hypothetical behaviour analysis interview concerning a serious crime. *Applied Cognitive Psychology, 27*(1), 60–70.

Meissner, C., Kelly, C., & Woestehoff, S. (2014). Improving the effectiveness of suspect interrogations. *Annual Review of Law & Social Science, 11*(1), 211–233.

Mendez, J. (2021). *Principles on effective interviewing for investigations and information gathering.* https://interviewingprinciples.com/

Milne, R. & Bull, R. (1999). *Investigative interviewing: Psychology and practice.* Chichester: Wiley.

Munsterberg, H. (1908). *On the Witness Stand: Essays on Psychology and Crime.* London: Forgotten Books.

Myklebust, T. (2009). *Analysis of field investigative interviews of children conducted by specially trained police investigators.* Unpublished PhD thesis. University of Oslo.

Myklebust, T. & Bjorklund, R. (2006). The effect of long-term training on police officers' use of open and closed questions in field investigative interviews of children (FIIC). *International Journal of Investigative Psychology and Offender Profiling, 3*, 165–181.

National Centre for Police Excellence. (2005). *Professionalising Investigation Programme, levels 1, 2, and 3.* Centrex: Wyboston.

Ofshe, R. & Leo, R. (1997). The social psychology of police interrogation. The theory and classification of true and false confessions. *Studies in Law, Politics and Society, 16*, 189–251.

Oxburgh, L., Gabbert, F., Milne, R., & Cherryman, J. (2016). Police officers' perceptions and experiences with MD suspects. *International Journal of Law and Psychiatry, 49*, 138–146.

Oxburgh, G., Myklebust, T., & Grant; T. (2010a). The question of question types in police interviews: A review of the literature from a psychological and linguistic perspective. *International Journal of Speech, Language and the Law, 17*, 45–66.

Oxburgh, G., Ost, J., & Cherryman, J. (2010b). Police interviews with suspected child sex offenders: Does use of empathy and question type influence the amount of investigation relevant information obtained? *Psychology, Crime and Law, 18*, 1–15.

Phillips, E., Oxburgh, G., & Myklebust, T. (2011). Investigative interviews with victims of child sexual abuse: The relationship between question and investigation relevant information. *Journal of Police and Criminal Psychology, 27*, 45–54.

Powell, M. & Snow, P. (2007). Guide to questioning children during the free-narrative phase of an investigative interview. *Australian Psychologist, 42*(1), 57–65.

Price, C. & Caplan, J. (1977). *The Confait confessions.* London: Boyars.

Rachlin, H. (2000). *The science of self-control.* London: Harvard University Press.

Shepherd, E. (2007). *Investigative interviewing: The conversation management approach.* Oxford: Oxford University Press.

Snook, B. & Keating, K. (2011). A field study of adult witness interviewing practices in a Canadian police organisation. *Legal and Criminological Psychology, 16*(1), 160–172.

Snook, B., Luther, K., Quinlan, H., & Milne, R. (2012). Let 'em talk! A field study of police questioning practices of suspects and accused persons. *Criminal Justice and Behaviour, 39*(10), 1328–1339.

Soukara, S., Bull, R., Vrij, A., Turner, M., & Cherryman, J. (2009). What really happens in police interviews of suspects? Tactics and confessions. *Psychology, Crime and Law, 15*, 493–506.

Stelfox, P. (2009). *Criminal Investigation: An introduction to principles and practice.* London: Willan.

Stewart, J., Woody, W., & Pulos, S. (2018). The prevalence of false confessions in experimental laboratory simulations: A meta-analysis. *Behavioural Sciences and the Law, 36*(1), 12–31.

Synnott, J., Dietzel., D., & Ioannou, M. (2015). A review of the polygraph: History, methodology, and current status. *Crime Psychology Review, 1*, 59–83.

Vrij, A. (2005). Cooperation of liars and truth tellers. *Applied Cognitive Psychology, 19*, 39–50.

Vrij, A., Fisher, R., & Blank, H. (2017). A cognitive approach to lie detection: A meta- analysis. *Legal and Criminological Psychology, 22*(1), 1–21.

Vrij, A., Mann, S., & Fisher, R. (2006). Information-gathering vs accusatory interview style: Individual differences in respondents' experiences. *Personality and Individual Differences, 41*, 589–599.

Vrij, A., Mann, S., Kristen, S., & Fisher, R. (2007). Cues to deception and ability to detect lies as a function of police interview styles. *Law and Human Behaviour, 31*, 499–518.

Walkley, J. (1987). *Police interrogation: A handbook for investigators.* London: Police Review Publication.

Walsh, D. & Bull, R. (2010). What really is effective in interviews with suspects? A study comparing interview skills against interviewing outcomes. *Legal and Criminological Psychology, 15*, 305–321.

Walsh, D. & Milne, R. (2008). Keeping the PEACE? A study of investigative interviewing practices in the public sector. *Legal and Criminological Psychology, 13*, 39–57.

Westera, N., Kebbell, M., & Milne, R. (2016). Want a better criminal justice response to rape? Improve police interviews with complainants and suspects. *Violence Against Women, 22*, 1–22.

Williamson, T. (2006). *Investigative interviewing: Rights, research, regulation.* Devon: Willan.

Williamson, T. (2007). Psychology and criminal investigation. In T. Newburn, T. Williamson, & A. Wright (Eds.), *Handbook of criminal investigation* (pp. 68–91). Cullompton: Willan.

Wright, A. & Alison, L. (2004). Questioning sequences in Canadian police interviews: Constructing and confirming the course of events? *Psychology, Crime and Law, 10,* 137–154.

Wright, R. & Powell, M. (2006). Investigative interviewers' perceptions of their difficulty to adhere to open-ended questions with child witnesses. *International Journal of Police Science and Management, 8,* 316–325.

2 The Concept of Vulnerability within the Criminal Justice System
What Does It Mean?

What Is Vulnerability?

Vulnerability within the criminal justice system (CJS) is not a new phenomenon (L. Oxburgh et al., 2016). Following the process of deinstitutionalisation, a large number of individuals are now treated within the community; it is a disproportionate number of these individuals that come into contact with the CJS (Sirdifield & Brooker, 2012). Despite vulnerability being a key concern across policing and public health partners (Murray et al., 2018) with increasing prioritisation being given to the identification, assessment, and management of vulnerable individuals in the CJS in England, Wales, and Scotland (College of Policing, 2018; Department of Health, 2014; Police Scotland, 2017), there does not appear to be a unified definition of vulnerability across policing, across public health, or within the policy documentation or literature. This has also been echoed across the international literature (Bull, 2010). This has led to vulnerability being defined in various ways. For example, vulnerability has been described as a state or condition whereby an individual is in danger, under threat, experiencing health challenges, at risk, and/or requiring support/protection (Larkin, 2009). This definition suggests that vulnerability is a dynamic state that can occur at any point in time. It also suggests that vulnerability is a very broad construct which makes it difficult when considering the development of assessment strategies and protocols within the CJS.

Academics have also attempted to define the concept of vulnerability. In a recent scoping review, international definitions of vulnerability were assessed in law enforcement and public health. Enang and colleagues (2019) reported fragmented definitions of vulnerability. They further highlighted that only four out of 34 articles reviewed provided explicit definitions of vulnerability – such definitions were based on the following:

DOI: 10.4324/9781003161028-2

(i)   Risk of death in vulnerable road users (Damsere-Derry et al., 2017)
(ii)   Social and physical risk environments (McNeil & Small, 2014)
(iii)   Being at risk of abuse, experience of abuse, being unable to take care of oneself or protect onself against exploitation (Whitelock, 2009)
(iv)   Being vulnerable due to age, level of intelligence quotient (IQ), and adaptive behaviour (Wilson, 2016)

As such, the scoping review highlighted the difficulties in identifying a universal definition of vulnerability.

Gudjonsson's Concept of Vulnerability

Although there is no universally agreed definition of vulnerability, Gudjonsson has extensively explored this area within academia for a number of years and defines vulnerability within the CJS as, "psychological characteristics or mental state which renders an [individual] prone, in certain circumstances, to providing information which is inaccurate, unreliable or misleading" (Gudjonsson, 2006, p.68). When considering psychological vulnerability, Gudjonsson (2018) identifies four main types:

(i)   Mental disorder: mental illness including mood disorders, schizophrenia, personality disorder, and learning disability
(ii)   Abnormal mental state: anxiety, intoxication, or withdrawal from alcohol and/or drugs
(iii)   Intellectual functioning: level of IQ
(iv)   Personality: psychological constructs including suggestibility, compliance, and acquiescence

Several studies have suggested the impact that an individual's level of vulnerability may have on the criminal investigation. For example, several field studies have consistently demonstrated a relationship between suggestibility and the likelihood to falsely confess (Gudjonsson, 2003, 2010, 2018). This has been echoed by more recent research that found that high levels of suggestibility and compliance are related to false confessions (Otgaar et al., 2020). Furthermore, those with mental health conditions and disorders, and juveniles are over-represented in proven false confession cases (Kassin et al., 2010). As such, consideration must be given to individual factors and the way that these may interact with the situation the individual may find themselves in when they enter the

CJS. The way that vulnerability is constructed within the CJS is particularly important.

Construction of Vulnerability in the Criminal Justice System

In considering vulnerability, the College of Policing has adopted the following definition: "a person is vulnerable if, as a result of their situation or circumstances, they are unable to take care of or protect themselves or others from harm or exploitation" (College of Policing, 2020, p.4). The College of Policing have produced recent guidelines that focus on supporting officers and staff when responding to vulnerable individuals. Consisting of one strategic-level guidelines for chief officers and three practical guidelines for police responders, the guidelines specify the actions that they should take to recognise, understand, and respond in situations with vulnerable individuals (College of Policing, 2020). Furthermore, the College of Policing has developed Authorised Professional Practice to assist officers when dealing with mental vulnerability and illness based on the National Decision Model. This includes gathering information and intelligence and guidance on how best to communicate with vulnerable individuals and provides web resources and publications to assist officers. Whilst these resources are undoubtfully helpful, it is the Police and Criminal Evidence Act (PACE, 1984) and Code C (2018) that provides requirements for the detention, treatment, and questioning of suspects, including those that are vulnerable, and the Youth Justice and Criminal Evidence Act (YJCEA, 1999) and Achieving Best Evidence in Criminal Proceedings (Ministry of Justice, 2011) that sets out guidance on how to interview victims and witnesses (herein referred to as witnesses) and guidance on how to use Special Measures for those that are intimidated or vulnerable.

Code C and the Vulnerable Suspect

Prior to 2018, and in addition to a juvenile, a suspect was considered vulnerable if an officer had any suspicion, or was told in good faith that the individual may be mentally disordered or otherwise mentally vulnerable and there was no clear evidence to dispel that suspicion (para 1.4, Code C, 2017). Suggested as the 'benefit of the doubt' test (Dehaghani & Bath, 2019), to treat the suspect as vulnerable only required a suspicion. What this meant was that the vulnerable suspect could receive the assistance of the necessary safeguards (such as the Appropriate Adult [AA]) without proof of vulnerability. However, following a public consultation by the Home Office in October 2017, significant revisions were made to Code C relating to the construction of vulnerability.

The revised Code C (2018) now no longer allows for exceptions for 17-year-olds and so all individuals under the age of 18 years are treated as juveniles. In addition, previously used terms such as "mentally disordered" and "mentally vulnerable" have been replaced with "vulnerable person." Paragraph 1.13(d) provides the following definition:

"Vulnerable" applies to any person who, because of a mental health condition or mental disorder:

(i) may have difficulty in understanding or communicating effectively about the full implications for them of any procedures and processes connected with:
  • their arrest and detention; or (as the case may be)
  • their voluntary attendance at a police station or their presence elsewhere for the purpose of a voluntary interview; and
  • the exercise of their rights and entitlements.
(ii) does not appear to understand the significance of what they are told, of questions they are asked or of their replies:
(iii) appears to be particularly prone to:
  • becoming confused and unclear about their position;
  • providing unreliable, misleading or incriminating information without knowing or wishing to do so;
  • accepting or acting on suggestions from others without consciously knowing or wishing to do so; or
  • readily agreeing to suggestions or proposals without any protest or question

Furthermore, Note 1G highlights that whilst a suspect may be vulnerable because of a mental health condition or mental disorder, an individual who does not have any such condition or disorder may still be considered vulnerable. Note 1G also indicates that consideration should be given to whether any of the factors listed in paragraph 1.13(d) may apply to the individual. In doing so, the particular circumstances of the individual, the nature of the investigation, and its impact should be taken into account when considering if that individual is vulnerable. It has been well documented that custody is a chaotic environment (Chariot et al., 2014), and scholars have suggested that any individual entering this environment could be considered vulnerable (Dehaghani

& Bath, 2019). The change in the definition of vulnerability thus reflects the impact of situational factors on the individual entering custody.

The change in the definition of vulnerability in Code C has attracted both positive and negative comments. There are now new actions required of police when identifying vulnerability – these include making reasonable enquiries regarding available information about an individual's potential vulnerability, keeping a record of what specified factors apply to the vulnerable suspect, and making that record available to the AA (para 1.4). In addition, the way that vulnerability is now considered reflects much of the academic literature in that concepts of suggestibility and compliance are alluded to, as are the impact of situational factors (see, e.g., Gudjonsson, 2018). In addition, some say that the revision amends what was a subjective test (suspicion) into a more objective one (reason to suspect) (National Appropriate Adult Network [NAAN], 2018). However, others highlight that the definition of vulnerability is considerably more complex and requires an increased threshold as it might exclude circumstances where an officer has 'suspicion' but cannot identify a specific factor (NAAN, 2018). Furthermore, it places an expectation on officers to be able to understand how different mental health conditions and disorders may map across the specific factors identified (Dehaghani & Bath, 2019). This raises concerns given recent work that suggests vulnerability is not always interpreted the way it should be (Farrugia, 2021). Whilst police officers can 'screen' for vulnerability, they are not clinical experts (Dehaghani & Bath, 2019). Consequently, the impact of the new definition on vulnerable suspects is yet to be seen.

Achieving Best Evidence and the Vulnerable Witness

Vulnerable witnesses are defined by Section 16 of the YJCEA, 1999 (as amended by the Coroners and Justice Act 2009). In addition to individuals under the age of 18 years (Section 16[1]), three other types of vulnerable witness are identified (Section 16(2)). These are:

(i)   Witnesses who have a mental disorder as defined by the Mental Health Act 1983 (as amended by the Mental Health Act 2007)
(ii)   Witnesses significantly impaired in relation to intelligence and social functioning (witnesses who have a learning disability)
(iii)   Witnesses who have a physical disability

Furthermore, 'intimidated' witnesses are defined by Section 17 as those whose quality of evidence is likely to be diminished by reason of fear or distress. Despite such individuals being identified as vulnerable and intimidated, they are only eligible for Special Measures to assist them to give their evidence if the quality (completeness, coherence, and accuracy) of their evidence is likely to be diminished by reason of the disorder or disability (Section 16[1][b]). As such, being able to access Special Measures is based on three 'tests' (Section 19):

(i)   Is the witness vulnerable or intimidated as defined by Sections 16 and 17?
(ii) Will any of the Special Measures or any combination of them likely improve the quality of the witness's evidence?
(iii) Which of the Special Measures are most likely to maximise the quality of the witness's evidence?

Special Measures include giving evidence at Court via the use of screens (Section 23), via the use of a TV link (Section 24), or in private (Section 25). Furthermore, the removal of wigs and gowns can be requested (Section 26) and the witness' video-recorded interview can be used as evidence-in-chief (Section 27). Vulnerable witnesses may also access the expertise of an intermediary (Section 29) and use communication aids (Section 30). In addition to the YJCEA (1999), Achieving Best Evidence in Criminal Proceedings (Ministry of Justice, 2011) provides guidance on interviewing victims and witnesses, and using Special Measures. Adopting the definitions of vulnerable and intimidated witnesses as outlined in the YJCEA, the Achieving Best Evidence document also provides extensive guidance about how to plan and prepare an interview, conduct the interview, and support and prepare the witness prior to Court and during their evidence at Court. Thus, whilst similar to Code C (2018) for vulnerable suspects in that Code C provides some understanding as to the impact of vulnerability on the suspects' evidence, the Achieving Best Evidence document provides extensive guidance on the following:

- Recognising vulnerable witnesses (e.g., characteristics of some syndromes) – para 2.60–2.72
- Planning and conducting the interview, with consideration given to the free narrative account – para 3.24–3.28
- Questioning – para 3.35–3.66
- Use of visual aids – para 3.103–3.122
- Special interviewing techniques – para 3.1233.129

In addition, the Achieving Best Evidence document considers the impact of race, gender, culture, and ethnic background and other life experiences that may impact upon the quality of the witness's evidence (see, e.g., para 2.111). Such depth of guidance is in stark contrast to that provided in Code C (2018) for vulnerable suspects. Here, the interpretation of vulnerability is subjective, and thus, the treatment of a vulnerable suspect is dependent on whom they encounter within the CJS. Subsequently, attention must be paid to the way in which these vulnerable individuals are perceived by those who have authority over their treatment and detention, especially those with mental health conditions or disorders, given the stigma this label often still evokes.

Perceptions of Suspects with Mental Health Conditions and Disorders

Criminalisation Hypothesis

Categorised as one type of psychological vulnerability (Gudjonsson, 2018), mental disorder can be defined as "any disorder or disability of the mind" (Mental Health Act, 2007). It is estimated that over 20% of police time is spent responding to individuals with mental health conditions or disorders with prevalence rates of those within custody far surpassing the level of mental illness in the general community (McKinnon & Grubin, 2013, 2014). One suggested reason for this is known as the criminalisation hypothesis (Abrahamson, 1972). This term has been used to describe the overrepresentation of individuals with mental health illness in the CJS (Ringhoff et al., 2012) and has long been viewed as an unanticipated side effect of deinstitutionalisation (Fisher et al., 2006). This hypothesis, then, essentially suggests that those with mental illness become entangled in the CJS because the community resources they need are often not available or are limited or inadequate (Peterson et al., 2010). Such vulnerable individuals move from the medical system into the CJS because of untreated mental illness.

Although the criminalisation hypothesis drives much of the contemporary policy related to suspects and offenders with mental health conditions or disorders (Skeem et al., 2010), there is a growing body of literature that challenges this assumption. Early research has suggested that the strongest risk factors for crime and recidivism are shared by offenders with and without mental health conditions or disorders (Fisher et al., 2006) and that arrests due to mental ill health account for only 8% of offenders with mental illness (Junginger et al., 2006). In more recent work, researchers found limited support for the criminalisation hypothesis. Peterson et al. (2010) found that in their sample of offenders with serious mental health illness, criminal behaviour was only occasionally a direct result of mental health symptoms – for example, in 5% of cases, criminal behaviour resulted from hallucinations and delusions. They suggest that only a minority of those with mental health conditions or disorders fit into the criminalisation hypothesis. Further work indicates a substantial number of inconsistent findings which has led to some suggesting that criminal justice outcomes are not strongly related to clinical factors (Case et al., 2009). For example, Case and colleagues (2009) highlighted that other non-clinical risk factors, such as a prior criminal history, may be more important than the individual's mental health in predicting subsequent arrests.

Other research suggests that those with mental health conditions or disorders are more likely to be arrested for minor offences, are less likely to be granted bail, and spend longer periods of time in police custody (Cummins, 2007; McNeil & Binder, 2007). This echoes early studies that suggest that when arrest rates are analysed in those with mental ill health and those without, the former are at an increased risk of being arrested than the latter (Teplin, 1984). More recently, work assessing the causal link between mental illness and crime has found that mental illness is correlated with factors that cause crime such as criminal thinking and that mental ill health elevates risk factors that lead to crime such as substance abuse (Frank & McGuire, 2010). Thus, some scholars acknowledge that there is convincing evidence of a small connection between individuals with mental health conditions and disorders and crime, although it is suggested that the connection is specific to only certain subsets of individuals with specific illnesses (Frank & McGuire, 2010; Ringhoff et al., 2012).

Psychological Theories

Unfortunately, suspects with mental health conditions or disorders are often perceived by many as dangerous and unpredictable (Daff & Thomas, 2014) and are considered to be responsible for a disproportionate level of serious and violent crime (Neumann & Hare, 2008) whilst presenting a greater risk of criminal recidivism (Douglas et al., 2006). Research regarding the treatment of such suspects within the CJS is mixed, however. Some suggest that when a suspect is believed to have a mental health condition or disorder, they are likely to receive a more serious use of force and are associated with an increased risk of violence compared to those with no mental health conditions or disorders (Charette et al., 2011; Chen et al., 2013; Johnson, 2011; Kesic & Thomas, 2014; Watson et al., 2014). However, other research has found that police officers were more likely to demonstrate an eagerness to assist individuals that have mental health conditions or disorders, were more likely to display empathy and a need for collaborative working with mental health services (McLean & Marshall, 2010). Furthermore, Watson and her colleagues (2004a, 2004b) found that the presence of a mental health condition had no effect on a police officer's proposed response to a hypothetical scenario – findings that have since been echoed in more recent work (McTackett & Thomas, 2017). Such mixed findings can be explained by several psychological theories that explore how perceptions influence subsequent interactions.

Schema Theory (Anderson, 1977) suggests that individuals develop schemas and stereotypes of groups of individuals that subsequently guide future interactions (Mayer et al., 1993). Such schemas can be influenced by the level of experience that an individual has (Psarra et al., 2008). For example, Watson et al. (2014) highlighted that police officers often develop frames of reference or 'schemas' shaped by their socialisation and experiences, for understanding and responding to situations involving those with mental health conditions or disorders.

Other psychological theories highlight that should an individual with a mental health condition or disorder be labelled as dangerous and violent, then it is likely that they will be stigmatised and treated as such (Noga et al., 2015). Conceptualised as Labelling Theory (Link et al., 1999; Scheff, 1984), if an individual is labelled negatively, then the way that they are treated may be different in comparison to the way in which those who do not have mental health conditions or disorders are treated due to the set of myths, stereotypes, or beliefs that the mental health label can evoke (Krameddine et al., 2013). Given that Labelling Theory suggests that it is professionals, including police officers, who enforce boundaries and thus are often the main source of labelling (Chambliss, 1973), the way in which individuals with mental health conditions or disorders are treated is heavily dependent on whom they encounter within the CJS.

An increasing body of research has been conducted generally on police officers' perceptions towards those with mental health conditions or disorders. However, very little has focused on the impact of such perceptions regarding this type of suspect within the investigative interview and the subsequent impact this may have on the interactions between the police officer and the vulnerable suspect. The work of Oxburgh and colleagues attempts to fill this gap.

Police Officers' Perceptions and Experiences with Mentally Disordered Suspects (Oxburgh et al., 2016)

Aims

The purpose of this study was to explore the perceptions of police officers when interviewing suspects with mental health conditions or disorders. The following research questions were addressed:

(i)   What perceptions do police officers have regarding suspects with mental health conditions or disorders they have interviewed and how have their experiences interviewing this vulnerable group impacted upon their perceptions?

(ii) What perceptions and experiences do police officers have in relation to support provided to suspects with mental health conditions or disorders?

(iii) What experiences do police officers have of current police training in mental health?

Method

Ethical approval was gained from the University of Portsmouth and from the Association of Chief Police Officers (ACPO).

Sample

Six police forces covering a large geographical area of England and Wales, including two large metropolitan police forces, registered their interest in participation. The sample was obtained via a purposive sampling method with the following inclusion criteria: trained to at least Professionalising Criminal Investigative Programme (PIP) Level 2 and experience of interviewing a suspect with a mental health condition or disorder within the previous 0–24 months. Given the qualitative nature of the research, recruitment of participants continued until data saturation was reached to ensure that the sample selected was representative. A total of 35 questionnaires were included for data analysis (24 male and 11 female participants). Participants had a mean age of 42 years and a mean length of police service of 17.29 years. The majority of all participants were Detective Constables ($n = 31$), with a few working as Detective Sergeant ($n = 2$), and a few as an Interview Advisor ($n = 2$). Participants reported that they had conducted a mean number of 19.37 investigative interviews in the previous 24 months, and of those, 3.03 involved a suspect with a mental health condition or disorder. The most commonly reported mental health conditions in suspects was depression (mean of 2.29 interviews conducted), followed by anxiety disorder (mean of 0.71), personality disorder (mean of 0.69), and schizophrenia (mean of 0.14). The majority of participants indicated that the most recent interview training completed had been PIP Level 3 ($n = 23$), but nearly half of the participants indicated that they had not received any mental heath training ($n = 15$) which would be expected at PIP Level 2.

Materials

A questionnaire consisting of 30 questions was developed containing a mixture of open and probing questions, such as, 'Please describe what you believe a mental disorder is' and 'Describe the most memorable investigative interview you have conducted with a suspect who has a mental disorder.' All questions were developed through identifying gaps within the current literature base and guidance and through piloting and liaising with serving police officers.

Procedure

Following the pilot, the questionnaire was disseminated to participants for completion through a key research contact at each participating police force. Participants were provided with an information sheet and consent form prior to the questionnaire. Participants returned their completed questionnaire to the researcher electronically.

Design

A qualitative design was adopted to allow for rich and in-depth data to be collected. Given the nature of the study, Grounded Theory (Glaser, 1978) was utilised for data analysis following an objectivist approach. This method is commonly used when little is known about the area of interest and allows for the construction of theories that are 'grounded' in the data itself (Charmaz, 2006) in order to explain the findings (Willig, 2008).

Data Analysis

Following the return of the completed questionnaires, all data were subjected to Grounded Theory analysis. Following an extensive reading of each questionnaire, each line of the raw data was labelled during which memos were recorded – this assisted in the development of the initial codes being raised to 'tentative' categories. Axial coding then took place, which involved condensing and synthesising the initial codes and categories in order to explain larger segments of the data. As potential relationships within the data started to emerge, the process of theoretical coding resulted in categories being weaved together to form a theory that explained the overall experience of the participants. Any disconformatory cases were worked into the emerging theory. In addition, the researcher employed an independent researcher to analyse a random sample of 15 questionnaires using the same Grounded Theory approach. Any discrepancies were discussed and resolved.

Results

Overall, nine conceptual categories with 21 subcategories emerged from the data – see Table 2.1. A brief summary is provided below but see Oxburgh et al. (2016) for a full description.

Table 2.1 Emergent conceptual categories and subcategories within the Police Experience Transitional Model (PETM)

Grouping	Conceptual Category	Subcategory	
1. Interviewee centred	1.1 Understanding and perceptions of mental disorder	(i)	What is mental disorder
		(ii)	Crime involvement of suspect groups
		(iii)	Mentally disordered suspects' presentation
	1.2 Communication difficulties in mental disorder	(i)	Communication barriers

(*continued*)

Table 2.1 Cont.

Grouping	Conceptual Category	Subcategory
		(ii) Communication attempts
		(iii) Importance of rapport
	1.3 Cognition level and subsequent assistance	(i) Impact on cognition
		(ii) Assistance in cognition
2. Interview centred	2.1 Emphasis and importance of investigation relevant information (IRI)	(i) Method of gathering IRI
		(ii) Impact of no IRI
	2.2 Impact of question type on behaviour and cognition	(i) Impact and use of open questions
		(ii) Impact and use of closed questions
	2.3 Use and impact on time	(i) Effective use and amount of time
		(ii) Stressors on time
3. Interviewer centred	3.1 Appropriateness of Person-Centred Approach (PCA) and Communication Accommodation Theory (CAT)	(i) Instances of PCA/CAT
		(ii) Non-committal to PCA/CAT
	3.2 Interviewer experience and perception of safeguards	(i) Impact of experience on interviewer understanding
		(ii) Interview familiarity and pressure
		(iii) Perceptions of current and new safeguards
	3.3 Current and future training perceptions	(i) Perceptions of current training
		(ii) Indications of future training

1. Interviewee Centred

1.1 UNDERSTANDING AND PERCEPTIONS OF MENTAL DISORDER

The majority of participants described mental disorder within a medical context by making references to specific mental disorders, psychological issues, and states of mind and disease. Other participants defined it within a social context by making reference to social norms and deviant behaviour, "when a person displays mannerisms not considered to be the norm" (participant 10). Misperceptions of mental health were also demonstrated. Participants also provided negative portrayals of suspects with mental health conditions and disorders. Such vulnerable suspects were described as uncooperative, with instances of labelling evident.

1.2 COMMUNICATION DIFFICULTIES IN MENTAL DISORDER

Some participants indicated that there were difficulties in communicating with suspects with mental health conditions and disorders during the police interview. This included the vulnerable suspect having a poor level of speech and a lack of understanding. However, the perceptions regarding communication difficulties were dependent on police officer experience. A keenness to engage with suspects with mental health conditions and disorders was reported, however, and reference was made to the level of rapport developed being positively related to the amount of information obtained during the interview: "I find that if you don't engage in the right way the planning will count for nothing and the remaining elements will be hugely affected" (participant 29).

1.3 COGNITION LEVEL AND SUBSEQUENT ASSISTANCE

Participants highlighted that the investigative interview can be dictated by the vulnerable suspects' capacity to understand, although this was not shared by the less experienced participants. It was commonly reported that suspects with mental health conditions and disorders have low-performing cognitive levels and a lack of responsibility in relation to the crime committed: "They don't believe they have done anything wrong...they're unaware of the seriousness of some offences" (participant 33). Despite this, participants indicated a desire to assist with their understanding during the interview process. Some suggested the use of communication tools and providing in-depth explanations within the interview. Participants reported that this increased the levels of engagement and rapport, resulting in more information being obtained.

2. Interview Centred

2.1 EMPHASIS AND IMPORTANCE OF INVESTIGATION RELEVANT INFORMATION

Some participants acknowledged that gaining an account from a suspect with a mental health condition or disorder can be problematic and not always achievable. Participants also perceived the amount of information gained from the interview as a measure of being an effective interviewer, although this tended to be expressed by the more experienced participants. Suspects with mental health conditions and disorders were reported to provide brief or confusing accounts in stark contrast to non-vulnerable suspects, who were perceived to be more cooperative: "They want to give their side of events across…they are keen to explain what they have or haven't done and why" (participant 3).

2.2 IMPACT OF QUESTION TYPE ON BEHAVIOUR AND COGNITION

Participants reported that open questions are the most frequently used when interviewing any type of suspect given the free and uninfluenced recall they encourage. However, other participants stated that these types of questions can be problematic for suspects with mental health conditions and disorders given the lack of boundaries and/or vague or irrelevant recall sometimes obtained. As such, some participants indicated how closed questions could be used in an appropriate manner – for example, using closed questions to retain some control or assisting the vulnerable suspects' understanding: "More specific or closed questions are easier to understand" (participant 1). Although there was a general consensus that open questions are best practice, the more experienced participants indicated that open questions are actually *inappropriate* when interviewing such vulnerable suspects.

2.3 USE AND IMPACT ON TIME

Participants regularly referred to the amount of time needed to deal with suspects with mental health conditions or disorders and how effective use of time is important to their own workload pressures and the investigation. Participants reported using time effectively in allowing regular breaks and shorter interviews when dealing with vulnerable suspects: "The interview was conducted in 15- to20-minute stages to allow the individual sufficient time to recover" (participant 29). However, the impact on the custody clock was reported, and so whilst allowing enough time to assist vulnerable suspects was reported as important, participants also reflected upon the impact this can have on the overall investigation.

3. Interviewer Centred

3.1 APPROPRIATENESS OF PERSON-CENTRED APPROACH AND COMMUNICATION ACCOMMODATION THEORY

When reporting on their own interview practice, over half of the participants reported that they would adopt a person-centred approach (PCA) when interviewing a suspect with a mental health condition or disorder. Reference was made to being open-minded and flexible in changing their approach to assist with understanding. This was evident in the more experienced participants. However, some participants questioned the flexibility and indicated that they would not change their behaviour when interviewing a vulnerable suspect: "Why deviate your style or approach" (participant 27).

3.2 INTERVIEWER EXPERIENCE AND PERCEPTION OF SAFEGUARDS

The majority of participants highlighted using their own personal experiences of mental illness when planning interviews with vulnerable suspects. Others referred to using the internet to learn about a specific mental health condition or disorder. All participants provided some insight into their perceptions of current safeguards such as AAs. Perceptions were mixed; the more experienced participants reported negativity whereas the least experienced participants tended to favour the positive contribution that such safeguards could offer. The impact of the participants' experience is concluded by one participant: "When I first joined you would not question the wisdom of the FME or custody nurse, who would say that the defendant is fit for interview and are 'well' when on occasions they clearly have mental health problems. I am far more cautious now" (participant 20).

3.3 CURRENT AND FUTURE TRAINING PERCEPTIONS

Nearly half of all participants indicated that they had not received any mental health training despite being actively involved in interviewing suspects with mental health conditions and disorders. The majority of participants provided some insight into what future training could entail. In addition to understanding mental health conditions and disorders, and effective questioning techniques, participants reported a desire for an experiential style of training, "I would like more input from medical professionals explaining different disorders and symptoms etc. and how to assist" (participant 11). Interestingly, the more experienced participants perceived the mental health training to be adequate, despite some of them not recording the completion of any such training courses.

Police Experience Transitional Model

All participants reported their perceptions and insight into their experiences and current practice when assisting with suspects with mental health conditions and disorders. Although some perceptions were very similar, there were some differences. These emerging differences may be explained by the variable levels of experience the participants had – that is, how many interviews they had conducted with this type of vulnerable suspect. Grounded within Schema Theory, the Police Experience Transitional Model (PETM; see Figure 2.1) indicates that the level of experience that

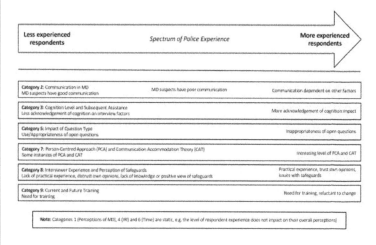

Figure 2.1 Police Experience Transitional Model (Oxburgh et al., 2016)

the police officer has may impact upon their current perceptions. In addition, the PETM suggests that the perceptions of police officers are not entirely static, that is, that their perceptions change as their level of experience does.

Summary

Vulnerability is a key concern across policing and public health partners (Murray et al., 2018) especially given the increasing number of vulnerable individuals entering the CJS. However, there does not yet appear to be one unified definition of what constitutes vulnerability. Current legislation provides some guidance to those dealing with vulnerable suspects and vulnerable witnesses, with recent changes to the definition of vulnerability within Code C (2018). However, regardless of such legislative guidance, research suggests that those with mental health conditions or disorders may still be perceived as dangerous and unpredictable. Concepts including the criminalisation hypothesis are still debated and other psychological theories indicate how individuals may develop schemas that drive interactions with individuals with mental health conditions or disorders; such vulnerable individuals are regularly labelled due to the set of myths, stereotypes of beliefs that the mental health label can evoke.

Although there is an increasing body of research that has explored police officers' perceptions towards those with mental health conditions and disorders, very little has focused on the impact of these perceptions within the investigative interview context. Oxburgh et al. (2016) analysed qualitative questionnaires that explored this. Overall, such vulnerable suspects were generally still viewed more negatively when compared to suspects without any vulnerability. Some participants indicated that they would change their approach to suit the needs and level of understanding of this type of suspect, and others questioned the rationale for doing so. Perceptions regarding the type of questioning strategy and the effectiveness of current safeguards were also reported. Such variable perceptions were conceptualised by the PETM. This suggests that the treatment and outcomes of suspects with mental health conditions or disorders is heavily dependent on whom they encounter and their perceptions (Cant & Standen, 2007).

Key Learning Points

- Vulnerable individuals are increasingly coming into contact with the CJS.
- Although there is no unified definition of vulnerability, Gudjonsson's concept of vulnerability identifies four main types of psychological vulnerability.
- Vulnerability is dynamic and includes individual and situational factors.
- The PACE (1984) and Code C (2018) provides requirements for the detention, treatment, and questioning of vulnerable suspects. It is the YJCEA (1999) and Achieving Best Evidence in Criminal Proceedings (Ministry of Justice, 2011) that provides legislative guidance for vulnerable and intimidated witnesses.
- The criminalisation hypothesis and other psychological theories can provide some explanation as to why individuals with mental health conditions and disorders are perceived negatively, although the research base is mixed.
- Recent work exploring police perceptions of such vulnerable suspects suggests that experience is a key factor in a police officer's schema.
- Suspects with mental health conditions and disorders are still viewed more negatively than their non-vulnerable counterparts, although officers recognise the need to engage with, build rapport, and interview according to the vulnerable suspects' needs.
- The treatment of a suspect with mental ill health is heavily dependent on whom they encounter in the CJS.

References

Abrahamson, M. (1972). The criminalisation of mentally disordered behaviour: A possible side effect of a new mental health law. *Hospital and Community Psychiatry*, *23*, 101–105.

Anderson, R. (1977). The notion of schemata and the educational enterprise: General discussion of the conference. In R. Anderson, R. Spiro, & W. Montague (Eds.), *Schooling and the acquisition of knowledge* (pp. 415–432). Hillsdale, MI: Erlbaum.

Bull, R. (2010). The investigative interviewing of children and other vulnerable witnesses: Psychological research and working/professional practice. *Legal and Criminological Psychology*, *15*, 5–23.

Cant, R. & Standen, P. (2007). What professionals think about offenders with learning disabilities in the criminal justice system. *British Journal of Learning Disabilities*, *35*, 174–180.

Case, B., Steadman, H., Dupis, S., & Morris, L. (2009). Who succeeds in jail diversion programs? A multi-site study. *Behavioural Sciences and Law*, *27*(5), 661–674.

Chambliss, W. (1973). The saints and the roughnecks. *Society*, *11*, 24–31.

Charette, Y., Crocker, A., & Billette, I. (2011). The judicious judicial dispositions juggle: Characteristics of police interventions involving people with a mental illness. *The Canadian Journal of Psychiatry*, *56*(11), 677–685.

Chariot, P., Lepresle, A., Lefevre, T., Boraud, C., Barthes, A., & Tedlaouti, M. (2014). Alcohol and substance screening and brief intervention for detainees kept in police custody. A feasibility study. *Drug and Alcohol Dependence*, *134*, 235–241.

Charmaz, K. (2006). *Constructing grounded theory: A practical guide through qualitative analysis*. London: Sage.

Chen, C., Jian-Jun, O., Jian-Song, Z., Ying-Dong, Z., Wei-Xiong, C., & Xiao-Ping, W. (2013). The comparison of disposal attitudes towards forensic psychiatric patients among police officers, psychiatrists and community members in China. *Journal of Forensic and Legal Medicine*, *20*, 986–990.

College of Policing. (2018). *Mental health: Mental health vulnerability and illness*. www.app.college.police.uk/appcontent/mental-health/ mental-vulnerability and illness/

College of Policing. (2020). *National vulnerability action plan (NVAP) revised 2020–2022*. National Police Chiefs' Council.

Cummins, I. (2007). Boats against the current: Vulnerable adults in police custody. *The Journal of Adult Protection*, *9*(1), 15–24.

Daff, E. & Thomas, S. (2014). Bipolar disorder and criminal offending: A data linkage study. *Social Psychiatry and Psychiatric Epidemiology*, *49*, 1985–1991.

Damsere-Derry, J., Palk, G., & King, M. (2017). Road accident fatality risks for "vulnerable" versus "protected" road users in northern Ghana. *Traffic Injury Prevention*, *18*(7), 736–743.

Dehaghani, R. & Bath, C. (2019). Vulnerability and the appropriate adult safeguard: Examining the definitional and threshold changes within PACE code C. *Criminal Law Review*, *3*, 213–232.

Department of Health. (2014). *The Mental Health Crisis Care Concordat: Improving Outcomes for People Experiencing Mental Health Crisis*. London: HMSO.

Douglas, K., Vincent, G., & Edens, J. (2006). Risk of criminal recidivism: The role of psychopathy. In C. Patrick (Ed.), *Handbook of psychopathy* (pp. 533–554). New York: Guildford Press.

Enang, I., Murray, J., Dougall, N., Wooff, A., Heyman, I., & Aston, E. (2019). Defining and assessing vulnerability within law enforcement and public health organisations: A scoping review. *Health and Justice*, *7*, 1–13.

Farrugia, L. (2021). Identifying vulnerability in police custody: Making sense of information provided to custody officers. *Journal of Forensic and Legal Medicine*, *80*, 102169.

Fisher, W., Silver, E., & Wolff, N. (2006). Beyond criminalisation: Toward a criminologically informed framework for mental health policy and services research. *Administration and Policy in Mental Health and Mental Health Services Research, 33*(5), 544–557.

Frank, R. & McGuire, T. (2010). *Mental health treatment and criminal justice outcomes.* www.nber.org/papers/w15858

Glaser, B.G. (1978). *Theoretical sensitivity. Advances in the methodology of grounded theory.* Mill Valley, CA: Sociology Press.

Gudjonsson, G. (2003). The psychology of interrogations and confessions: A handbook. Chichester: Wiley.

Gudjonsson, G. (2006). The psychological vulnerabilities of witnesses and the risk of false accusations and false confessions. In A. Heaton-Armstrong, E. Shepherd, G. Gudjonsson, & D. Wolchover (Eds.), *Witness testimony. Psychological, investigative and evidential perspectives* (pp. 61–75). Oxford: Oxford University Press.

Gudjonsson, G. (2010). Psychological vulnerabilities during police interviews: Why are they important? *Legal and Criminological Psychology, 15*(2), 161–175.

Gudjonsson, G. (2018). *The psychology of false confessions: Forty years of science and practice.* West Sussex: Wiley.

Home Office. (1984). *Police and Criminal Evidence Act and Codes of Practice (2018).* London: Home Office.

Johnson, R. (2011). Suspect mental disorder and police use of force. *Criminal Justice and Behaviour, 38*, 127–145.

Junginger, J., Claypoole, C., Ranilo, I., & Crisanti, A. (2006). Effects of serious mental illness and substance abuse on criminal offences. *Psychiatric Services, 57*(6), 879–882.

Kassin, S., Drizin, S., Grisso, T., Gudjonsson, G., Leo, R., & Redlich, A. (2010). Police induced confessions: Risk factors and recommendations. *Law and Human Behaviour, 34*, 3–38.

Kesic, D. & Thomas, S. (2014). Do prior histories of violence and mental disorders impact on violent behaviour during encounters with police? *International Journal of Law and Psychiatry, 37*, 409–414.

Krameddine, Y., Demarco, D., Hassel, R., & Silverstone, P. (2013). A novel training programme for police officers that improves interactions with mentally ill individuals and is cost-effective. *Front Psychiatry, 4*(9), 1–10.

Larkin, M. (2009). *Vulnerable groups in health and social care.* London: Sage.

Link, B., Phelan, J., Bresnahan, M., Stueve, A., & Pescosolido, B. (1999). Public perceptions of mental illness: Labels, causes, dangerousness, and social distance. *American Journal of Public Health, 89*, 1328–1333.

Mayer, J., Rapp, H., & Williams, U. (1993). Individual differences in behavioural prediction: The acquisition of personal-action schemata. *Personality and Social Psychology Bulletin, 19*, 443–451.

McKinnon, I. & Grubin, D. (2013). Health screening of people in police custody evaluation of current police screening procedures in London, UK. *European Journal of Public Health, 23*(3), 399–405.

McKinnon, I. & Grubin, D. (2014). Evidence-based risk assessment screening in police custody: The HELP-PC study in London, UK. *Policing, 8*(2), 174–182.

McLean, N. & Marshall, L. (2010). A front line police perspective of mental health issues and services. *Criminal Behaviour and Mental Health, 20*, 62–71.

McNeil, D. & Binder, R. (2007). Effectiveness of a mental health court in reducing criminal recidivism and violence. *American Journal of Psychiatry, 163*(9), 1395–1403.

McNeil, R. & Small, W. (2014). Safer environment interventions: A qualitative synthesis of the experiences and perceptions of people who inject drugs. *Social Science and Medicine, 106*, 151–158.

McTackett, L. & Thomas, S. (2017). Police perceptions of irrational unstable behaviours and use of force. *Journal of Police and Criminal Psychology, 32*, 163–171.

Mental Health Act. (1983). London: HMSO

Mental Health Act. (2007). London: HMSO.

Ministry of Justice. (2009). *Coroners and Justice Act 2009.* www.legislation.gov.uk/ukpga/2009/25/contents

Ministry of Justice. (2011). *Achieving best evidence in criminal proceedings: Guidance on interviewing victims and witnesses and using special measures.* London: HMSO.

Murray, J., Heyman, I., Wooff, A., Dougall, N., Aston, L., & Enang, I. (2018). *Law enforcement and public health: Setting the agenda for Scotland.* Scottish Institute for Policing Research Annual Review.

National Appropriate Adult Network. (2018). *PACE Update: Changes to Code C, E, F, and H.*

Neumann, C. & Hare, R. (2008). Psychopathic traits in a large community sample: Links to violence, alcohol use, and intelligence. *Journal of Consulting and Clinical Psychology, 76*, 893–899.

Noga, L., Walsh, E., Shaw, J., & Senior, J. (2015). The development of a mental health screening tool and referral pathway for police custody. *The European Journal of Public Health, 25*(2), 237–242.

Otgaar, H., Schell-Leugers, J., Howe, M., Villar, A., Houben, S., & Merckelbach, H. (2020). The link between suggestibility, compliance and false confessions: A review using experimental and field studies. *Applied Cognitive Psychology, 35*, 445–455.

Oxburgh, L., Gabbert, F., Milne, R., & Cherryman, J. (2016). Police officers' perceptions and experiences with MD suspects. *International Journal of Law and Psychiatry, 49*, 138–146.

Peterson, J., Skeem, J., Hart, E., Vidal, S., & Keith, F. (2010). Analysing offence patterns as a function of mental illness to test the criminalisation hypothesis. *Psychiatric Services, 61*(12), 1217–1222.

Police Scotland. (2017). *Policing 2026: Our 10 year strategy for policing in Scotland.* www.scotland.police.uk/assets/pdf/138327/ 386688/policing-2026-strategy.pdf

Psarra, V., Sestrini, M., Santa, Z., Petsas, D., Gerontas, A., Garnetas, C., & Kontis, K. (2008). Greek police officers' attitudes towards the mentally ill. *International Journal of Law and Psychiatry, 31*, 77–85.

Ringhoff, D., Rapp, L., & Robst, J. (2012). The criminalisation hypothesis: Practice and policy implications for persons with serious mental illness in the criminal justice system. *Best Practices in Mental Health, 8*(2), 1–19.

Scheff, T. (1984). *Being mentally ill.* Piscataway, NJ: Aldine Transaction.

Sirdifield, C. & Brooker, C. (2012). Detainees in police custody: Results of a health needs assessment in Northumbria, England. *International Journal of Prisoner Health, 8*, 60–67.

Skeem, J., Manchak, S., & Peterson, J. (2010). Correctional policy for offenders with mental illness: Creating a paradigm for recidivism reduction. *Law and Human Behaviour, 35*(2), 110–126.

Teplin, L. (1984). Criminalising mental disorder: The comparative arrest rates of the mentally ill. *American Psychologist, 39*(7), 794–803.

Watson, A., Corrigan, P., & Ottati, V. (2004a). Police officers' attitudes toward and decisions about persons with mental illness. *Psychiatric Services, 55*, 49–63.

Watson, A., Corrigan, P., Ottati, V. (2004b). Police responses to persons with mental illness: Does the label matter? *The Journal of the American Academy of Psychiatry and the Law, 32*, 378–385.

Watson, A., Swartz, J., Bohrman, C., Kriegel, L., & Draine, J. (2014). Understanding how police officers think about mental/emotional disturbance calls. *International Journal of Law and Psychiatry, 37*, 351–358.

Whitelock, A. (2009). Safeguarding in mental health: Towards a rights-based approach. *The Journal of Adult Protection, 11*(4), 30–42.

Willig, C. (2008). *Introducing qualitative research methods in psychology: Adventures in theory and method.* Maidenhead: McGraw Hill Open University Press.

Wilson, C. (2016). Victimisation and social vulnerability of adults with intellectual disability: Revisiting Wilson and Brewer (1992) and responding to updated research. *Australian Psychologist, 51*(1), 73–75.

Youth Justice and Criminal Evidence Act. (1999). London: HMSO.

3 The Vulnerable Suspect and the Criminal Justice System

Identification, Safeguards, and Diversion

Individuals with mental health conditions and disorders are over-represented in custody in England and Wales (Fazel & Seewald, 2012; McKinnon & Grubin, 2010). Research has indicated that between 33% and 63% of those detained in custody have mental health conditions or disorders (McKinnon & Grubin, 2014). Such prevalence rates are echoed around the world (see, e.g., Chariot et al., 2014 and Dorn et al., 2014). Thus, individuals in custody have much higher levels of mental ill health when compared to the general population (Dorn et al., 2014), and this is a worldwide concern (Fazel & Seewald, 2012; Heide et al., 2012).

Identification of Vulnerable Adult Suspects: Current Guidance

Internationally, police responses and custody procedures vary when identifying vulnerable suspects (McKinnon et al., 2016). In England and Wales, it is the Police and Criminal Evidence Act (PACE, 1984) and the associated Codes of Practice that provides the legal framework under which custody services operate. Upon arrival into custody, the suspect will undergo a 'booking in' procedure that involves being asked a number of questions as part of a risk assessment by a custody officer (McKinnon & Grubin, 2013). Whilst the first national risk assessment guidance was produced in 2000 (Police Leadership and Powers Unit, 2000), advice has continued to evolve to incorporate recommendations following investigations into deaths in custody (Hannan et al., 2010). Subsequently, the increasing robustness of the risk assessment has been acknowledged as a contributing factor into the reduction of deaths in custody in recent years (Angiolini, 2017). Currently, the risk assessment contains questions relating to the individuals' physical and mental health (see Table 3.1).

Current Authorised Professional Practice (APP) guidance states that the custody officer is responsible for documenting and recording the

DOI: 10.4324/9781003161028-3

Table 3.1 Risk assessment questions from the Authorised Professional Practice guidance

---

Main Questions

How are you feeling in yourself now?

Do you have any illness or injury?

Are you experiencing any mental ill health or depression?

Would you like to speak to the doctor/nurse/paramedic (as appropriate)?

Have you seen a doctor or been to a hospital for this illness or injury?

Are you taking or supposed to be taking any tablets or medication? If yes, what are they and what are they for?

Are you in contact with any medical or support service? If yes, what is the name of your contact or support worker there?

Do you have a card that tells you who to contact in a crisis?

Have you ever tried to harm yourself? If yes, how often, how long ago, how did you harm yourself, have you sought help?

Supplementary questions should the detainee answer yes to any of the above.
What is the name of your general practitioner (GP) and GP's surgery?

Do you have a family member who is aware of your health problems?

Is there anything I can do to help?

Source: College of Policing (2017).

risk assessment for every individual brought into custody in accordance with Code C, paragraphs 3.6–3.10. This includes (but is not limited to) conducting the risk assessment to obtain information about the detainee that is relevant to their safe custody (para 3.6), responding appropriately to any specific risk identified (para 3.9), and continuously reviewing the risk assessment if circumstances should change (para 3.10). Whilst there is no standard risk assessment model for police in England and Wales, the conducting of risk assessments should be guided by the National Decision Model.

The purpose of the risk assessment is to identify the level of risk the individual may pose to themselves or others and whether a healthcare professional or an Appropriate Adult (AA) is required (Brooker et al., 2018; National Appropriate Adult Network [NAAN], 2015). Subsequently, individuals will be placed on one of four predefined observation levels (College of Policing, 2017). These are documented in Table 3.2.

The College of Policing highlights that all officers should receive appropriate training and demonstrate a basic understanding when dealing with vulnerable individuals including those that may have a mental health condition or disorder. Subsequently, a range of resources that focus on recognising and responding to vulnerability have been developed to support officers to better recognise individuals at risk of harm, the vulnerabilities that they may encounter, and how to interact effectively with vulnerable individuals (College of Policing, 2020). Furthermore, the College of Policing has developed APP that focuses

Table 3.2 Observation levels from the Authorised Professional Practice guidance

Observation Level	Requirements
Level 1 – General observation	Minimum acceptable level of observation. Detainee is checked hourly.
Level 2 – Intermittent observation	Minimum level of observation for detainees under the influence of alcohol and/or drugs. Detainees visited every 30 minutes and roused.
Level 3 – Constant observation	Used when there is a heightened level of risk. Detainee under constant observation (usually through CCTV) and visited every 30 minutes. Detainee reviewed by a healthcare professional.
Level 4 – Close proximity	Used for detainees at highest risk of harm. Detainees are physically supervised in close proximity. Detainee reviewed by a healthcare professional.

Source: College of Policing (2017).

on a range of strategic considerations relating to vulnerability (see College of Policing, 2016a). Thus, the amount of guidance and APP has rapidly developed in recent years.

Problems in Identification of Vulnerability in Adult Suspects

Despite the implementation of recent guidance and APP , identifying the vulnerabilities of suspects in custody remains problematic (Baksheev et al., 2012; Gudjonsson, 2010; Kassin, 2012; McKinnon & Grubin, 2013; Noga et al., 2015). A number of reasons have been identified. Many individuals who have mental health conditions or disorders may mask their vulnerabilities due to the social stigma it can evoke (Herrington & Roberts, 2012). Whilst custody officers are expected to identify vulnerability, the risk assessment relies on the self-reporting of suspects entering custody. Subsequently, this can impact upon the accuracy of the assessment as it is unlikely that all suspects will disclose information about their mental health (Bradley, 2009).

Secondly, the screening tools that custody officers currently use in England and Wales are arguably not 'fit for purpose' – that is, they do not fully identify the breadth and depth of vulnerabilities that suspects may present with upon entering custody (McKinnon & Grubin, 2013, 2014; Young et al., 2013). Indeed, the current risk assessment is known to miss many cases of mental illness (McKinnon & Grubin, 2013) with suggestions that only 52% to 63% of those with mental health conditions or disorders and learning disabilities are identified.

Third, despite regular and ongoing contact with vulnerable individuals, custody officers receive very little to no formal training in mental health (Bather et al., 2008). This adds to the ambiguity regarding the definition and understanding of vulnerability given that the risk assessment may vary between police forces with some adding their own questions to supplement the guidance (Stoneman et al., 2018). Additionally, some scholars suggest that the evaluation of risk is subjective, based on the custody officers' judgement and experience (Stoneman et al., 2019). Thus, there still remains some difficulties in the identification of vulnerability in those that enter custody.

Vulnerability in the Criminal Justice System: Implementing Safeguards

When a vulnerable suspect is identified, they are entitled to a number of safeguards to assist them as they progress through the custody process. In addition to clinical attention and assessment from a forensic medical examiner or custody nurse, the vulnerable suspect is also entitled to an AA.

The Vulnerable Suspect and the Appropriate Adult

The role of the AA is defined within Code C (2018) as a parent, guardian, or other person responsible for the vulnerable suspect's care or custody. In the absence of such individuals, an AA can be any other responsible adult aged 18 years and above who is not a police officer or otherwise employed by the police (para 1.7). The role of the AA is to safeguard the rights, entitlements, and welfare of juveniles and vulnerable suspects. As such, the AA is expected to support, advise, and assist the vulnerable suspect in relation to the Codes of Practice and the custody processes in which they may be required to participate; observe whether the police are acting properly and fairly; assist the vulnerable suspect with communication with the police; and ensure that they understand their rights and that those rights are protected and respected (para 1.7A).

Although current guidance indicates that a parent or guardian should be considered in the first instance (College of Policing, 2020), it has been suggested that they do not understand or perform the role well. For example, in early research, Evans (1993) found that in 74.8% of interviews where parents were acting as an AA, they made little or no contribution. When parents do contribute, however, their interventions are consistent with control or punishment (Brown, 1997; Bucke & Brown, 1997). Other parents were reported to have tried to assist the police in obtaining a confession (Dixon et al., 1990). As such, many observations of parents acting as AAs show that their level of contribution is minimal or inappropriate (Pierpoint, 2001). It must be noted, however, that parents may not be able to identify, for example, when an interview is being conducted unfairly (Irving & McKenzie, 1989).

Consequently, organised groups of trained individuals carry out this role. Described as a professional AA, such individuals volunteer or are employed within an AA scheme (NAAN, 2015) and have no connection with or prior knowledge of the vulnerable suspect (Pierpoint, 2011). The use of professional AAs was recommended over 20 years ago by the Home Office (1995) and has since been encouraged in more recent years (Pierpoint, 2004). Schemes that utilise professional AAs tend to be organised and funded locally; however, the NAAN is the national membership body supporting and representing organisations delivering AA support.

Despite the introduction of the AA safeguard and the increasing provision of professional AA schemes, there remains some problems with the implementation of this safeguard (Bradley, 2009; NAAN, 2015). An early study reported that only 58% of "psychologically vulnerable" suspects had been interviewed with the use of an AA (Medford et al., 2003); this has been supported by more recent research (e.g., Young et al., 2013). In addition, there appears to be a lack of consistency in the use of AAs across police force areas. For example, Bath and Dehaghani (2020) found significant differences in the recorded rate – Sussex Police reported that 25.2% of cases required an AA in comparison to Northumbria Police and West Midlands who reported 2.35% and 0.72% respectively. This suggests that an individual's vulnerability and the need for an AA may be detected in one police force but not necessarily in another. Furthermore, concerns relating to the suitability, availability, and quality of the AA have been well documented (NAAN, 2015; NAAN, 2019; Oxburgh et al., 2016). Dehaghani (2019) found that there are specific barriers to the implementation of the AA for a vulnerable adult suspect. These included the severity of the crime – those who had been arrested for less serious offences would not necessarily be provided with an AA, and the type of vulnerability identified. In her research, she reported that those with autism were not always provided with an AA if they were perceived to be intelligent and articulate, and mental health conditions, such as depression and schizophrenia, were not considered serious enough to warrant an AA. She further reported that an AA would only be deemed necessary if the suspect had issues with capacity, knowledge, and understanding, despite the presence of a mental health condition or disorder. This suggests that even when vulnerability is identified, implementing the appropriate safeguards remains a subjective decision (McKinnon & Finch, 2018). The way in which custody officers make sense of information provided to them when making such decisions and thus implementing the appropriate safeguards was explored further in the work of Farrugia (2021).

Identifying Vulnerability in Police Custody: Making Sense of Information Provided to Custody Officers (Farrugia, 2021)

Aims

The purpose of this study was to understand how custody officers in England and Wales make sense of different types of information presented to them and the impact that it has on their initial judgments of vulnerability and subsequent implementation of safeguards. The following research questions were addressed:

(i)   How do custody officers make use of different types of information presented to them in identifying vulnerability?
(ii)   What impact does this have upon their responses?
(iii) Is there a difference in police force area?

Given previous work, the following hypotheses were generated:

H1. There will be a difference in custody officer response dependent on the type of vulnerability presented to them.
H2. Custody officers will be more likely to seek the expertise of an AA where the suspect has comprehension difficulties.
H3. There will be a difference in response based on police force area.

Method

Ethical approval was gained from the Human Research Ethics Committee of the University of Sunderland.

Sample

The sample was obtained using a purposive and snowball sampling method. The author's key research contacts were utilised to recruit participants from police forces in England and Wales with the following inclusion criteria; participant was a custody officer, they had been in their role for a minimum of three months, and the questionnaire was fully completed. In total, 288 participants completed the questionnaire; 52 incomplete responses were excluded resulting in a final sample of 237 participants from 25 police forces in England and Wales (see Table 3.3). No other demographic information was obtained.

Materials

Case scenario vignettes relating to an individual brought into custody on suspicion of a crime were developed. With the assistance of a serving police officer, the vignettes were designed to recreate the type and nature of information that a custody officer would receive upon an individual entering custody in a real-life scenario. Each case scenario contained standardised details relating

Table 3.3 Participation from police force areas

Police Force Area	Participating Police Force	N
North of England	Cleveland	1
	Durham	5
	Northumbria	50
	North Yorkshire	1
	Total	57
Midlands	Cambridgeshire	2
	Cheshire	8
	Derbyshire	2
	Greater Manchester	1
	Humberside	2
	Staffordshire	3
	Total	18
South West/Borders/West	Avon and Somerset	7
	Devon and Cornwall	20
	Dyfed-Powys	12
	Gloucestershire	10
	Gwent	2
	South Wales	24
	West Mercia	15
	Wiltshire	6
	Total	96
South East	Bedfordshire	3
	Hertfordshire	6
	Kent	6
	Met	29
	Surrey	7
	Sussex	10
	Thames Valley	5
	Total	66
Overall Total		237

Source: Farrugia (2021).

to the crime (a male arrested on suspicion of a violent crime), but elements relating to the individual's vulnerability differed and were designed to trigger reference to the relevant safeguards under the PACE (1984) and Code C (2018), for example, having a mental health condition or displaying comprehension difficulties. Each element was based on those documented in the literature as having an impact on the decision-making of custody officers in interpreting vulnerability. After each vignette, disposal options currently available to custody officers in England and Wales were presented in order to capture the initial decision that a custody officer would make. The case scenario vignettes were hosted and disseminated via Qualtrics.

Procedure

Participants were required to read an information sheet and provide consent thus confirming they met the inclusion criteria. Each of the six case scenario vignettes and the subsequent disposal options were presented in a random order. After reading each vignette, participants were required to indicate which disposal option they would opt for based on the vulnerabilities displayed by the individual in each case scenario. Following the completion of all six case scenario vignettes, participation was completed, and the data were analysed.

Design

A 4 (Police Force Area: North of England vs Midlands vs South West/Borders/Wales vs South East) × 6 (Scenario: no vulnerability vs mental health but no symptoms and full comprehension vs no mental health but presence of symptoms and full comprehension vs mental health and medication and full comprehension vs mental health but no medication and full comprehension vs mental health but no symptoms and comprehension difficulties) within-subjects design was used, with the dependent variable consisting of the type of disposal option: (i) straight to cell and an immediate interview; (ii) straight to cell and a delayed interview; (iii) the use of an AA; (iv) a mental health assessment from a custody nurse/other professional; and (v) request the suspect receives medical attention at hospital.

Data Analysis

Analyses were performed using SPSS software (IBM SPSS Statistics for Mac, version 24.0). Data analyses included tests of significance such as chi-square tests and loglinear analysis. First, chi square tests were performed to compare the type of case scenario vignettes and the disposal options. Secondly, a loglinear analysis was conducted to compare police force area, case scenario vignettes, and disposal options. The differences were considered significant for *p* values < .05.

Results

Case Scenario and Disposal Options

A chi-square test was conducted to examine the relationship between the case scenario and the disposal option. There was a significant relationship between the type of case scenario and the disposal outcome, $\chi^{2(15)} = 808.20$, $p < .001$. Cohen's (1969) effect size ($d = 0.44$) suggests a medium practical significance. Custody officers were more likely to obtain a mental health assessment from a nurse or other healthcare professional in all case scenarios regardless of type of vulnerability, except if the individual displayed comprehension difficulties. See Figure 3.1.

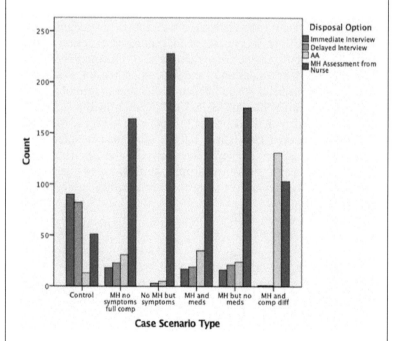

Figure 3.1 Graphical representation of the relationship between the type of case scenario and the disposal outcome (Farrugia, 2021)

Police Force Area, Case Scenario, and Disposal Options

The type of disposal options custody officers would choose based on the police force area in addition to the case scenario type was also examined. A three-way loglinear analysis produced a final model that retained all effects. The likelihood ratio of this model was $\chi^2 (0) = 0$, $p = 1$. This indicated that the highest-order interaction (police force area × disposal option and case scenario × disposal option) was significant, $\chi^2 (84) = 788.90$, $p < .001$.

To break down this effect, a separate chi-square test on the disposal option was performed for each of the police force areas. There was a significant association between the disposal option and the police area, $\chi^2 (9) = 19.86$, $p = .02$. All police force areas were most likely to obtain a mental health assessment for the vulnerable suspect. However, whilst the second most likely disposal option was obtaining the assistance of an AA, this was only the case for three police force areas; police forces in the North of England were instead likely to opt for a delayed interview. Differences in the third most likely and the least likely disposal options between police force areas were also observed. This suggests fundamental differences in the disposal options preferred between police force areas (see Table 3.4). However, Cohen's (1969) effect size value ($d = 0.07$) suggests a low practical significance.

Table 3.4 Association between police force area and disposal option

Police Force Area	Disposal Option				
	Immediate Interview	Delayed Interview	Appropriate Adult	MH Assessment	Total
North of England	10.20%	15.20%	14.70%	59.90%	100.00%
Midlands	8.30%	5.60%	13.00%	73.10%	100.00%
South West / Borders / Wales	8.70%	9.20%	18.10%	64.00%	100.00%
South East	12.20%	9.70%	18.10%	60.00%	100.00%

Source: Farrugia (2021).

The Vulnerable Suspect and the Intermediary

The intermediary is one of a package of Special Measures allowed to assist vulnerable witnesses in the Youth Justice and Criminal Evidence Act (YJCEA, 1999). It allows for vulnerable witnesses to have their examination conducted through an intermediary; the intermediary's role is to communicate

> questions put to the witness, and to any persons asking such questions, the answers given by the witness in reply to them, and to explain such questions or answers so far as necessary to enable them to be understood by the witness or person in question.
>
> (section 29(2))

Intermediaries, in this capacity, are not witness supporters or expert witnesses, but rather impartial, owing their duty to the court (section 29(5)).

The first intermediaries were recruited in 2003. Whilst section 29 of the YJCEA (1999) created the role of the intermediary, it did not identify who should perform it. Thus, the Home Office recruited a cohort of intermediaries with relevant professional skills who had to undergo and successfully complete a training course and police criminal record check in order to achieve registration within this role. Intermediaries were provided with a Code of Practice, Code of Ethics, and a guidance manual to enact their role (Ministry of Justice, 2020) and were placed on a register managed by the Home Office. Requests for intermediaries sought to match the skillset of the intermediary to the needs of the vulnerable witness. Following the evaluation of Home Office pilot schemes in 2004 and 2005, a national rollout of the intermediary scheme was recommended and immediately accepted in 2006 by the Home Office (Plotnikoff & Woolfson, 2015). The National Crime Agency now hosts the intermediary register matching vulnerable witnesses with Registered Intermediaries, the majority of requests being made by the police or the Crown Prosecution Service. Vulnerable witnesses are now assisted at each stage of the criminal justice process, from the initial investigative interview through to pretrial preparations and giving evidence at trial.

The term 'Registered Intermediary' is restricted to those recruited by the Ministry of Justice and who assist vulnerable witnesses as per the requirements of the YJCEA (1999). As vulnerable suspects and defendants are excluded from this Act (Section 17(1)), they are not eligible to access a Registered Intermediary via the matching service and the national register (Plotnikoff & Woolfson, 2015). This is also the case even when judges exercise their inherent jurisdiction to appoint an intermediary for a defendant, despite many defendants meeting the criteria for the provision of Special Measures.

Although suspects and defendants are excluded from the YJCEA (1999), an amendment added by s.104 of the Coroners and Justice Act (2009) considers examination of the accused through an intermediary and provides a direction as per Section 33BA:

> for any examination of the accused to be conducted through an interpreter or other person approved by the court for the purposes of this section ("an intermediary").
>
> (Para 3)

Furthermore, Section 33BA describes that the function of an intermediary is to communicate questions put to the defendant and the answers given in reply, as well as explain any such questions or responses to enable them to be understood (para 4).

Unfortunately, this amendment is yet to come into force, and even where direction is provided by the judge to allow for an intermediary, the lack of access to a matching service (in the same way as exists for a Registered Intermediary) makes it difficult to find a suitable defendant intermediary. In reality, those who take on defendant work are likely to already be working as a Registered Intermediary with vulnerable witnesses and thus also willing to take on defence cases or are professionals working exclusively with defendants. Indeed, there are private sector organisations – Communicourt, Triangle, and Intermediaries for Justice – that recruit and train intermediaries for vulnerable defendants (Plotnikoff & Woolfson, 2015).

Having an intermediary assist a defendant is a contentious issue. It is usual practice where an intermediary has been appointed that this will be only for when the defendant provides their evidence rather than the duration of the trial. This has been heavily criticised – see *R (AS) v Great Yarmouth Youth Court* [2011] EWHC 2059 (Admin), para 6, for example – where courts have recognised that without the appropriate assistance throughout the duration of the trial, the defendant would not be able to have a fair trial. However, more recently, the Divisional Court directed that it is not essential for an intermediary to be present to assist the defendant for the duration of the trial given that outside of the defendant giving their evidence, their needs could be met by general support, reassurance, and calm interpretation (*R (OP) v Secretary of State for Justice* [2014] EWHC 1944 (Admin), para 41). It should also be noted that an intermediary to assist a vulnerable suspect during the investigative interview is very rare.

Diversion Out of Custody: Liaison and Diversion Services

The criminal justice system (CJS) has not always catered well for vulnerable individuals. Quite often, those with mental health conditions or disorders only access the relevant care services when they have been arrested and thus enter the CJS. As such, liaison and diversion (L&D) services aim to improve the health and criminal justice outcomes where a range of complex needs are identified as factors in the offending behaviour. Thus, L&D is the process in which vulnerable individuals are identified and assessed as early as possible and then diverted away from the CJS and towards relevant health and social care services that can support their needs (College of Policing, 2016b).

L&D services are a relatively new concept. Following a number of reviews from 2007, the Bradley Report (2009) set out recommendations for vulnerable individuals in the CJS. Amongst the reforms, the review called for all police custody suites to have access to L&D services designed to a common national model rather than the ad hoc models and coverage that had been in existence for the previous 25 years. As such, in 2008, a number of organisations, including the Department of Health, the Ministry of Justice, and the Home Office, supported a major national programme involving six pilot youth justice L&D schemes for vulnerable juveniles. The aim was to identify and support such vulnerable individuals into services as early on as possible in their contact with the youth justice system (Haines et al., 2012). In 2009, the government committed to developing a delivery plan and launched the 'Improving Health, Supporting Justice: The national delivery plan of the Health and Criminal Justice Programme Board.' This included commitments to improve mental health support for those in contact with the CJS and develop care pathways that ensured that individuals were diverted away from the formal youth justice system (Petrosino et al., 2010). The development and delivery of a national model for L&D services was also central to the plan.

Since the introduction of several initiatives (see, e.g., the Mental Health Crisis Care Concordat, HM Government 2014), the 'Liaison and Diversion Operating Model' was launched and implemented in 2014 at ten trial sites in England, followed by a further 13 sites in 2015. The National Model provides 24-hour, seven-days-a-week services for all individuals in the adult and youth justice pathways and covers individuals who have a range of vulnerabilities, including mental health, physical health, and learning disabilities (NHS England Liaison and Diversion Programme, 2014). Key elements of the National Model focus not only on identification and screening but appropriate assessment, referral if required, and outreach work. The roll-out of NHS England–commissioned L&D services achieved 100% coverage across England in early 2020 (NHS, 2020).

Does Liaison and Diversion Work?

L&D services are not underpinned by a strong evidence base, despite attracting significant national funding (Kane et al., 2020). One systematic review identified that whilst L&D services were generally seen as a positive addition to services, the actual impact of these services on mental health outcomes and reoffending had been subjected to methodologies that were only moderately rigorous and not to high-quality research studies (Scott et al., 2013). Such findings have been documented in further recent reviews (Kane et al., 2018) with some scholars indicating the need for future research and funding strategies to build in high-quality, systematic evaluation of outcomes before implementing a theoretically attractive strategy more widely (Schucan & Shemilt, 2019). Other more recent work found a strong positive correlation between the L&D interventions and changing offending behaviour and improvement in at least one critical area of mental health outcome, thus reducing mental health act sections for individuals (Kane et al., 2020).

A recent outcome evaluation of the National Model for L&D services (Disley et al., 2021) reported that the L&D services that follow the National Model have succeeded in engaging with vulnerable individuals who have a broad range of difficulties. For example, 71% of those referred had a mental health condition or disorder, with 20% recorded as having more than one mental health need. The outcome evaluation also found that L&D services appear to intervene at a point of crisis but that the interventions offered vary by individual and by site. However, this is documented as a planned aspect of the National Model given that referrals and other interventions should be tailored to individual needs. Other findings include a short-term increase in referral to mental health services. But other results have also suggested that a referral to L&D services does not appear to reduce reoffending, although it does appear to increase diversion from custodial sentences and overall contributes to savings in the CJS.

Summary

Given the prevalence rate of individuals with mental health conditions and disorders in custody, the need for appropriate and effective identification of such vulnerabilities is critical. The current risk assessment in England and Wales attempts to identify vulnerability by asking questions relating to the individuals' physical and mental health. However, given that it is the custody officer who is responsible for conducting and documenting the risk assessment with vulnerable individuals in custody, the analysis and evaluation of risk can be considered subjective and based on the custody officers' judgment and own personal experience (Stoneman et al., 2019). Identifying vulnerability in custody remains problematic despite the implementation of recent guidance and APP. This is due to a number of reasons relating to disclosure from the vulnerable suspect, the ability of the screening tools designed to identify vulnerability, and the little to no formal training received by custody officers.

When vulnerability is identified, a number of safeguards should be implemented to assist the vulnerable suspect throughout their time in custody. One of these is the AA. Despite their role being defined in the PACE (1984), Code C (2018), there remains problems with implementing this safeguard. Generally, there is inconsistency in the way in which the AA is utilised within police forces in England and Wales (Farrugia, 2021), and even when vulnerability is identified, an AA is not always implemented. Factors such as severity of crime and severity of mental health condition or disorder appear to play a significant role, thus suggesting that this remains a subjective decision (McKinnon & Finch, 2018). Another safeguard that can be implemented is the use of the intermediary to assist the defendant at trial. Whilst this is legislated for vulnerable witnesses (YJCEA, 1999), suspects and defendants are excluded from this Act and an amendment is yet to be implemented (s.104, Coroners and Justice Act, 2009).

Vulnerable individuals entering the CJS may now be assisted by L&D services. This is the process by which vulnerable individuals who come into contact with the CJS can be diverted away and assisted to engage with health and social care services that can support their needs (College of Policing, 2016b). Such recommendations were set out by the Bradley Report in 2009; there now exists a National Model that provides 24-hour, seven-days-a-week services for all vulnerable individuals entering the CJS. However, research has been mixed as to its efficacy. Some suggest that there is a strong positive correlation between L&D interventions and changing offending behaviour, and improvements in mental health (Kane et al., 2020), whereas other suggest that it does not result in a reduction of reoffending behaviour (Disley et al., 2021). It appears, therefore, that whilst some progress has been made in identification, safeguards, and diversion, there remains more work to do to assist the vulnerable suspect in the CJS.

Key Learning Points

> - The over-representation of vulnerable suspects in custody is well documented in England and Wales and internationally.
> - The PACE (1984) and the associated Codes of Practice provide the legal framework under which custody services operate.
> - The custody officer is responsible for each detained person in custody including conducting the risk assessment.
> - There remain some difficulties in the identification of vulnerability and subsequent implementation of safeguards.
> - If vulnerability is identified, vulnerable suspects should have access to an AA. The use of an intermediary for suspects and defendants is yet to come into force and it is at the discretion of the judge.
> - Research has documented that custody officers are likely to choose a mental health assessment regardless of type of vulnerability, except if the individual displayed comprehension difficulties – here they are likely to opt for an AA.
> - The implementation of L&D services is in response to the 2009 review conducted by Lord Bradley; the aim is to identify and assess vulnerable individuals and then divert them away from the CJS and towards health and social care services that can support their needs.
> - Currently, there are mixed findings as to the success of L&D services.

References

Angiolini, E. (2017). *Report of the independent review of deaths and serious incidents in police custody*. London: Home Office.

Baksheev, G., Ogloff, J., & Thomas, S. (2012). Identification of mental illness in police cells: A comparison of police processes, the brief jail mental health screen and the jail screening assessment tool. *Psychology, Crime and Law*, *18*, 529–542.

Bath, C. & Dehaghani, R. (2020). *There to help 3. The identification of vulnerable adult suspects and application of the appropriate adult safeguard in police investigations in 2018/19*. London: National Appropriate Adult Network.

Bather, P., Fitzpatrick, R., & Rutherford, M. (2008). *Briefing 36: Police and mental health*. London: Sainsbury Centre for Mental Health.

Bradley, K. (2009). *The Bradley Report: Lord Bradley's review of people with mental health problems or learning disabilities in the criminal justice system*. London: Department of Health.

Brooker, C., Tocque, K., Mitchell, D., & Pearce, M. (2018). Police custody in the North of England: Findings from a health needs assessment in Durham and Darlington. *Journal of Forensic and Legal Medicine*, *57*, 91–95.

Brown, D. (1997). *PACE ten years on: A review of the research*. HORS 155. London: Home Office.

Bucke, T. & Brown, D. (1997). *In police custody: Police powers and suspects' rights under the revised PACE Codes of Practice*. HORS 174. London: HMSO.

Chariot, P., Lepresle, A., Lefevre, T., Boraud, C., Barthes, A., & Tedlaouti, M. (2014). Alcohol and substance screening and brief intervention for detainees kept in police custody. A feasibility study. *Drug and Alcohol Dependence*, *134*, 235–241.

Cohen, J. (1969). *Statistical power. Analysis for the behavioural sciences*. New York: Academic Press.

College of Policing. (2016a). *Mental health index*. www.app.college.police.uk/mental health-index-2/

College of Policing. (2016b). *Mental health and the criminal justice system*. www.app.college.police.uk/app-content/mental-health/crime-and-criminal justice/

College of Policing. (2017). *Detention and custody. Risk assessment*. www.app.college.police.uk/app-content/detention-and-custody-2/riskassessment/#content-of-risk-assessments

College of Policing. (2020). *Detention and custody. Children and young persons*. www.app.college.police.uk/app-content/detention-and-custody-2/detainee care/children-and-young-persons/#appropriate-adults

Dehaghani, R. (2019). *Vulnerability in police custody. Police decision-making and the appropriate adult safeguard*. London: Routledge.

Disley, E., Gkousis, E., Hulme, S., Morley, K., Pollard, J., Saunders, C., Sussex, J., & Sutherland, A. (2021). *Outcome evaluation of the national model for liaison and diversion*. Cambridge: RAND.

Dixon, D., Bottomley, C., Coleman, M., Wall, G., & Wall, D. (1990). Safeguarding the rights of suspects in police custody. *Policing and Society*, *1*, 115–140.

Dorn, T., Ceelan, M., Buster, M., Stirbu, I., Donker, G., & Das, K. (2014). Mental health and health-care use of detainees in police custody. *Journal of Forensic and Legal Medicine*, *26*, 24–28.

Evans, R. (1993). *The conduct of police interviews with young people*. Royal Commission on Criminal Justice Research Study No.8. London: HMSO.

Farrugia, L. (2021). Identifying vulnerability in police custody: Making sense of information provided to custody officers. *Journal of Forensic and Legal Medicine, 80,* 102169.

Fazel, S. & Seewald, K. (2012). Severe mental illness in 33,588 prisoners worldwide: Systematic review and meta-regression analysis. *The British Journal of Psychiatry, 200,* 364–373.

Gudjonsson, G. (2010). Psychological vulnerabilities during police interviews. Why are they important? *Legal and Criminological Psychology, 15,* 161–175.

Haines, A., Goldson, B., Haycox, A., Houten, R., Lane, S., McGuire, J., Nathan, T., Perkins, E., Richards, S., & Whittington, R. (2012). *Evaluation of the Youth Justice Liaison and Diversion (YJLD) Pilot Scheme. Final Report.* University of Liverpool.

Hannan, M., Hearnden, I., Grace, K., & Bucke, T. (2010). *Deaths in or following police custody: An examination of the cases 1998/99–2008/09.* London: Independent Police Complaints Commission.

Heide, S., Stiller, D., Lessig, R., Lautenschlager, C., Birkholz, M., & Fruchtnicht, W. (2012). Medical examination for fitness of police custody in two large German towns. *International Journal of Legal Medicine, 126,* 27–35.

Herrington, V. & Roberts, K. (2012). Addressing psychological vulnerability in the police suspect interview. *Policing, 6,* 1–10.

HM Government. (2014). *Mental health crisis care concordat: Improving outcomes for people experiencing mental health crisis.* London: Department of Health.

Home Office. (1984). *Police and Criminal Evidence Act (1984) and Codes of Practice (2018).* London: Home Office.

Home Office. (1995). *Appropriate adults: Report of review group.* London: HMSO.

Irving, B. & McKenzie, I. (1989). *Police interrogation: The effects of the Police and criminal Evidence Act.* London: Police Foundation of Great Britain.

Kane, E., Evans, E., Mitsch, J., & Jilani, T. (2020). Are liaison and diversion interventions in policing delivering the planned impact: A longitudinal evaluation in two constabularies? *Criminal Behaviour and Mental Health, 30,* 256–267.

Kane, E., Evans, E., & Shokraneh, F. (2018). Effectiveness of current policing-related mental health interventions: A systematic review. *Criminal Behaviour and Mental Health, 28*(2), 108–119.

Kassin, S. (2012). Why confessions trump innocence. *American Psychologist, 67,* 431–445.

McKinnon, I. & Finch, T. (2018). Contextualising health screening risk assessments in police custody suites – qualitative evaluation from the HELP-PC study in London, UK. *BMC Public Health, 18,* 393–406.

McKinnon, I. & Grubin, D. (2010). Health screening in police custody. *Journal of Forensic and Legal Medicine, 17,* 209–212.

McKinnon, I. & Grubin, D. (2013). Health screening of people in police custody – evaluation of current police screening procedures in London, UK. *The European Journal of Public Health, 23,* 399–405.

McKinnon, I. & Grubin, D. (2014). Evidence-based risk assessment screening in police custody: the HELP-PC study in London, UK. *Policing*, *8*, 174–182.

McKinnon, I., Thomas, S., Noga, H., & Senior, J. (2016). Police custody healthcare: A review of health morbidity, models of care and innovations within police custody in the UK, with international comparison. *Rick Management and Healthcare Policy*, *9*, 213–226.

Medford, S., Gudjonsson, G., & Pearse, J. (2003). The efficacy of the appropriate adult safeguard during police interviewing. *Legal and Criminological Psychology*, *8*(2), 253–266.

Ministry of Justice. (2009). *Coroners and Justice Act 2009*. www.legislation.gov.uk/ukpga/2009/25/contents

Ministry of Justice. (2020). *Registered Intermediary Procedural Guidance*. https://assets.publishing.service.gov.uk/government/uploads/system/uploads/attachmnt_data/file/955316/registered-intermediary-procedural-guidance-manual.pdf

National Appropriate Adult Network. (2015). *There to help: Ensuring provision of appropriate adults for mentally vulnerable adults detained or interviewed by police*. www.appropriateadult.org.uk/images/pdf/2015_theretohelpcomplete.pdf

National Appropriate Adult Network. (2019). *There to help 2*. https://appropriateadult.org.uk/policy/research/there-to-help-2

NHS England. (2014). Liaison and diversion operating model 2013/14. www.england.nhs.uk/commissioning/health-just/liaison-and-diversion/about/

NHS England. (2020). About liaison and diversion. www.england.nhs.uk/commissioning/health-just/liaison-and-diversion/about/

Noga, H., Walsh, E., Shaw, J., & Senior, J. (2015). The development of a mental health screening tool and referral pathway for police custody. *European Journal of Public Health*, *25*, 237–242.

Oxburgh, L., Gabbert, F., Milne, R., & Cherryman, J. (2016). Police officers' perceptions and experiences with MD suspects. *International Journal of Law and Psychiatry*, *49*, 138–146.

Petrosino, A., Turpin-Petrosino, C., & Guckenburg, S. (2010). Formal system processing of juveniles: Effects on delinquency. *Campbell Systematic Reviews*, *6*(1), 1–88.

Pierpoint, H. (2001). The performance of volunteer appropriate adults: A survey of call outs. *Howard Journal of Criminal Justice*, *40*(3), 255–271.

Pierpoint, H. (2004). A survey of volunteer appropriate adult services in England and Wales. *Youth Justice*, *4*(1), 33–45.

Pierpoint, H. (2011). Extending and professionalising the role of the appropriate adult. *Journal of Social Welfare and Family Law*, *33*(2), 139–155.

Plotnikoff, J. & Woolfson, R. (2015). *Intermediaries in the criminal justice system: Improving communication for vulnerable witnesses and defendants*. University of Bristol: Policy Press.

Police Leadership and Powers Unit. (2000). *Detainee risk assessment and revised prisoner escort record (PER form)*. Home Office. http://library.college.police. uk/docs/hocirc/ho-circ-2000-032-detainee-risk assessment-and-PER.pdf

R (AS) v Great Yarmouth Youth Court [2011] EWHC 2059 (Admin)

R (OP) v Secretary of State for Justice [2014] EWHC 1944 (Admin)

Schucan, K. & Shemilt, I. (2019). The crime, mental health, and economic impacts of prearrest diversion of people with mental health problems: A systematic review. *Criminal Behaviour and Mental Health, 29*(3), 142–156.

Scott, D., McGilloway, S., Dempster, M., Browne, F., & Donnelly, M. (2013). Effectiveness of criminal justice liaison and diversion services for offenders with mental disorders: A review. *Psychiatric Services, 64*(9), 843–849.

Stoneman, M., Jackson, L., Dunnett, S., & Cooke, L. (2018). Variation in detainee risk assessment within police custody across England and Wales. *Policing and Society, 29*(8), 951–967.

Stoneman, M., Jackson, L., Dunnett, S., & Cooke, L. (2019). Enhanced understanding of risk assessment in police custody in England and Wales using statistical modelling. *Safety Science, 117*, 49–57.

Young, S., Goodwin, E., Sedgwick, O., & Gudjonsson, G. (2013). The effectiveness of police custody assessments in identifying suspects with intellectual disabilities and attention deficit hyperactivity disorder. *BMC Medicine, 11*, 248–259.

Youth Justice and Criminal Evidence Act. (1999). London: HMSO.

4 The Role of the Appropriate Adult
Passivity v Intervention

Individuals entering custody will undoubtedly find the process daunting and stressful (Chariot et al., 2014; Newburn, 2013). When individuals have mental health conditions or disorders, the process may become exceptionally confusing and exacerbate their existing vulnerabilities (HM Inspectorate of Constabulary [HMIC], 2015). Research has documented the lack of understanding reported by vulnerable suspects of not only the custody process as a whole but the investigative interview with specific reference made to not knowing what to say or do when being interviewed by the police (Hyun et al., 2014). It has also been consistently reported that those with mental health conditions and disorders are at a heightened risk of falsely confessing to crimes (e.g., Gudjonsson, 2018). Given the inherent difficulties and vulnerabilities that those with mental health conditions and disorders face when entering custody, the role of one key safeguard, the Appropriate Adult (AA), plays an important part in assisting such vulnerable individuals (Heide & Chan, 2016).

Despite the implementation of the AA as per Code C (2018), the role has received little attention within the psychological literature and the efficiency of this safeguard is scarcely documented (Pierpoint, 2011). Some research has focused on ensuring the provision of AAs when vulnerable adults first enter custody (Cummins, 2007; McKinnon & Grubin, 2010). Other similar research has explored what constitutes an effective AA service, with a particular focus on availability and delays in securing services (Bath, 2014; Jessiman & Cameron, 2017; Pierpoint, 2000, 2006).

Of the minimal research that has explored the role of the AA, scholars have suggested that the AA tends to be passive in their role and does not intervene when required to ensure that the rights, entitlements, and welfare of vulnerable individuals are safeguarded (Evans, 1993; Pierpoint, 2001). This is concerning given the increased risk vulnerable

DOI: 10.4324/9781003161028-4

suspects are at when they enter custody. However, the role of the AA has continued to evolve and develop since its implementation, and there are increasing numbers of AA schemes that operate under the National Appropriate Adult Network (NAAN). Thus, the efficiency of the AA role warrants further exploration. This was explored in the work of Farrugia and Gabbert (2019).

The "Appropriate Adult": What They Do and What They Should Do in Police Interviews with Mentally Disordered Suspects (Farrugia & Gabbert, 2019)

Aims

The aim of this study was to explore the actions of AAs during police interviews conducted with suspects that have mental health conditions and disorders. The following research questions were addressed:

(i)   To what extent do AAs intervene during interviews conducted with suspects that have mental health conditions and disorders?

(ii) What (if any) missed opportunities were there for AAs to intervene during interviews conducted with suspects that have mental health conditions and disorders?

(iii) Are AA interventions appropriate and in line with the Police and Criminal Evidence Act (PACE, 1984), Code C (2018)?

In light of Evans (1993) and Pierpoint's (2001) research, the following hypothesis was generated:

H1. AAs will be more likely to remain passive during interviews conducted with suspects that have mental health conditions and disorders.

Despite the number of updates in Code C (2018), particularly the definition of vulnerability, those relating to the role of the AA have hardly changed and, in light of the period of data collection, police officers conducting the interviews in the current sample were using definitions relating to vulnerability prior to the change implemented in 2018.

Method

Ethical approval was gained from the Faculty of Humanities and Social Sciences at the University of Portsmouth. Furthermore, the first author was security-vetted in order to obtain the data. Interview transcripts were anonymised.

Sample

In total, five police forces were approached to provide samples of police interviews conducted with suspects that have mental health conditions and disorders implicated in a serious offence and in the presence of an AA. Overall, 28 interviews were received relating to the period of 2002–2015. The police interviews were included if (i) the vulnerable suspect provided an account to the interviewing officer; (ii) an AA was present; and (iii) the case was classified as closed. Consequently, one interview was excluded as although the suspect was recorded as having a mental health condition, the interview was conducted without the presence of an AA. The final sample of police interviews included in the present study was 27. Although all participating police forces had access to an AA scheme, it was unclear if the AAs involved in the interviews in this sample came from such a scheme, were other professionals working as AAs, or were relatives/guardians.

Materials

Based on the AA role defined in Code C, and previously reported research (e.g., Medford et al., 2003), a coding framework and guide was developed to assist in the analysis of the police interviews. The coding framework consisted of four sections: (i) general sample characteristics, including the demographics of the vulnerable suspect, the interviewing officers, and additional persons present, as well as the interview outcome; (ii) interventions made by the AA in the interview that fell within Code C – for example, ensuring that the vulnerable suspect understood their legal rights and caution, or assisting with communication, and were thus labelled as 'appropriate interventions'; (iii) interventions made by the AA that fell outside of their role as defined by Code C such as answering questions on behalf of the vulnerable suspect or adopting the role of the second interviewing officer and therefore labelled as 'inappropriate interventions'; and (iv) interventions that should have been made but were missed by the AA, thus labelled as 'missed interventions.'

Procedure

Following the reading of each interview, the first author systematically coded each utterance (or apparent lack of it) made by the AA based on the coding framework. Once all of the police interviews included in the sample were coded, an independent researcher (currently a serving police officer) was provided with the coding framework and guide and was instructed to code approximately 25% of the police interview data. Overall, an agreement level of 95% was achieved, indicating an excellent level of agreement between the two coders. The data were then analysed.

Design

A within-subjects design was used to measure (i) the number of actual interventions made by AAs during the police interviews conducted with suspects that have mental health conditions and disorders and whether these are appropriate interventions as per Code C and (ii) the number of 'missed' interventions by AAs – that is, occurrences where it would be reasonably expected that the AA would have intervened as per Code C.

Results

General Characteristics of the Police Interview Sample

Out of the 27 interviews included in the final sample, the majority of the suspects were male ($n = 21$) as were the main police interviewers ($n = 17$) and the second interviewer ($n = 20$). A Legal Advisor was present in the majority of the interviews ($n = 23$), and in a small number of the interviews, a mental health nurse ($n = 1$) and/or a doctor ($n = 1$) were also present in addition to the AA and the interviewers. Research has documented a similar gender distribution among suspects and interviewing officers, in addition to the likelihood of an attending Legal Advisor (Leahy-Harland, 2013; Soukara, 2004). In terms of the mental health conditions and disorders recorded on the custody database, the majority (n = 13) were recorded as having an unspecified mental health condition. However, five of the vulnerable suspects were recorded as having schizophrenia, two had other psychoses, three were recorded as having depression, two with dissociative identity disorder, one with anxiety, and one with borderline personality disorder. There was no indication within the custody records of comorbidity. The majority of the vulnerable suspects (n = 20) were being interviewed in relation to a murder or an attempted murder, with the other seven suspects being interviewed regarding sexual offences, including rape (n = 5), sexual assault against an adult (n = 1), and sexual assault against a child (n = 1). Twelve of the vulnerable suspects denied the offence, 12 made a full admission, and 3 vulnerable suspects provided a partial admission.

Appropriate versus Missed Interventions

Instances during the investigative interview when the AA intervened (appropriate interventions) were compared to missed interventions. AAs were significantly less likely to appropriately intervene (mean = 1.04, SD = 2.24) than they were to miss an opportunity to intervene (mean = 7.48, SD = 5.23), t = 6.44, p = .001; see also Table 4.1.

Table 4.1 Appropriate, inappropriate, and missed interventions

Type of Appropriate Adult (AA) Intervention	Mean	Standard Deviation
Appropriate		
Prompt officer to inform suspect of role and duties of AA	0.05	0.23
Explain interview process/use of Legal Advisor	0.04	0.19
Clarify decision re: use of Legal Advisor	0.04	0.19
Remind suspect of legal rights	0.07	0.39
Provide additional information to the Legal Advisor	0.07	0.27
Confirm role as an AA and not as a Legal Advisor	0.04	0.19
Inform officer of suspect misunderstanding of a question or the need for clarification	0.15	0.53
Encouraging suspect to take additional time to respond	0.04	0.19
Assist in explanation of drugs test	0.04	0.19
Assisting with CCTV	0.04	0.19
Inform officer of suspect distress (if not noted by the officer)	0.19	0.48
Highlighting the suspect requires a break	0.04	0.19

Table 4.1 Cont.

Type of Appropriate Adult (AA) Intervention	Mean	Standard Deviation
Confirmed case was not discussed in break	0.04	0.19
Inform officer the suspect is still awake	0.15	0.78
AA highlights own distress	0.04	0.19
Read witness statement to suspect	0.04	0.19
Sign witness statement on behalf of suspect	0.04	0.19
Read significant statement to suspect	0.04	0.19
Sign significant statement on behalf of suspect	0.04	0.19
Inappropriate		
Challenging the suspect account	0.04	0.19
Adopting the role of the officer, e.g., questioning the suspect	0.19	0.79
Providing an opinion on the suspect's mental health	0.07	0.39
Clarifying points of evidence	0.04	0.19
Missed		
Prompt officer to check suspect's understanding of legal rights	0.63	0.5
Prompt officer to check suspect's understanding of caution	0.26	0.45
Prompt officer to inform suspect of AA role and duties	0.16	0.38
Long interview/failure to ask for a break/not receiving a break when requested	0.67	1.04
Suspect misunderstanding of the question or the need for clarification	1.19	1.27
Officer requiring assistance in understanding suspect account	0.11	0.32
Requiring visual tool to assist understanding	0.19	0.48
Suspect appearing distressed/mental health issues not acknowledged	1.11	1.87
Inappropriate challenging from the officer	1.41	1.53
Constant interruption from the officer	0.04	0.19
Officer leading the suspect/suggesting responses	0.59	1.01
Suspect guessing in responses	0.74	1.16

Source: Farrugia and Gabbert (2019).

Inappropriate versus Missed Interventions

Instances during the investigative interview when the AA intervened when it was not necessary to do so were also compared with missed interventions – that is, instances when the AA would have been expected to intervene but did not. AAs were significantly less likely to intervene inappropriately (mean = 0.33, SD = 1.04) than they were to miss an opportunity to intervene (mean = 7.48, SD = 5.23), $t = 6.71$, $p = .001$.

Appropriate versus Inappropriate Interventions

The final analyses focused on whether the interventions made by the AA were deemed appropriate or inappropriate. When an AA did intervene, they were significantly more likely to be appropriate (mean = 1.04, SD = 2.24) than inappropriate (mean = 0.33, SD = 1.04), $t = 2.06$, $p = .05$; see also Table 4.1

Farrugia and Gabbert's (2019) study provides an interesting insight into the actual implementation of the AA role. Their results suggest that AAs frequently failed to intervene and that such missed opportunities were significantly more common than the AA making an intervention. However, their results also suggest that when AAs do intervene, it is more likely to be an appropriate intervention than an inappropriate one. Although research regarding the AA's role is limited, the findings from Farrugia and Gabbert (2019) mean that there are now three published studies that suggest the passivity of AA and so their findings fall in line with previous work (Evans, 1993; Pierpoint, 2001). It should be noted, however, that the AAs in Farrugia and Gabbert's (2019) sample could have been family members or trained AAs. This was not clear from the records obtained. This is important as research suggests that there are differences between family members fulfilling this role and trained AAs in the way in which the role is enacted (Evans, 1993; Medford et al., 2003). Regardless, it is important to raise awareness of these findings so that AAs receive the support they need to implement their role efficiently, whether they are family members or trained professionals. The passivity of the AA coupled with the complexities of the vulnerable suspect present clear challenges in the criminal justice system (CJS).

The Appropriate Adult Role: Their Perceptions

Several studies have now reported the passivity of AAs when performing their role (Evans, 1993; Farrugia & Gabbert, 2019; Medford et al., 2003). Surprisingly, very little research has explored how the AA experiences their role whilst working within custody. However, scholars have highlighted that the role of the AA is a complex, demanding, and confusing one (Bartlett & Sandland, 2003; Cummins, 2011). Others indicate how the AA role may have been socially constructed and that such perceptions differ depending on the role of the perception holder, for example, the legislator, the courts, the vulnerable suspect, the police, and the AAs themselves (Pierpoint, 2006). For example, the AA may view their role as a welfare role, or to ensure due process. Others may view it as a crime prevention role or a combination of all of these (Pierpoint, 2006). This has been documented consistently throughout the literature. For example, in one early study, Pierpoint (2006) highlighted that when AAs were provided with clear provisions, such as the right to request legal advice on behalf of a juvenile suspect, the AA tended to perform their role appropriately. However, when requirements of the role were more ambiguous, such as ensuring that interviews were being conducted fairly, AAs tended to impose their own interpretations and engaged in activities that fell outside of their role. Pierpoint also highlighted the subjective interpretation of the AA role with some police officers and parents considering the role to involve control. Such varying perceptions or confusion regarding the primary function of the AA role has been found in more recent research (Jessiman & Cameron, 2017).

Others suggest that it is not just the professionals involved in the CJS that are confused about the AA role but also those that carry out this role (HMIC, 2015). Early research reported that many AAs may not fully understand their role, may be compliant with or disempowered by the police, resulting in little or inappropriate interventions (Nemitz & Bean, 2001). Others suggest that little is known about how the AA constructs and understands their role (Miller, 2015). Overall, what is clear, however, is that the AA role is a complex but important one (Bath, 2014), and, given the passivity and critique of AAs reported in the literature, it is important to gain an understanding of how the AAs perceive, understand, and enact their role. Such understanding from the AAs' perspective could provide a unique insight into the complex role they play when assisting vulnerable individuals in custody. The work of Farrugia (submitted) attempts to do this.

The 'Professional' Appropriate Adult: Their Perspective (Farrugia, submitted)

Aims

The aim of this study was to explore how professionally trained AAs understand and perceive their role when working in custody with vulnerable individuals. As such, the following research questions were addressed:

(i)   How do AAs understand their role?
(ii) What are the lived experiences of AAs when they enact their role?
(iii) What impact does this have on their ability to enact their role when working in custody alongside other professionals and vulnerable suspects?

Method

Ethical approval was gained from the Human Research Ethics Committee of the University of Sunderland.

Sample

Organisations that recruit and train individuals as part of the NAAN were approached and provided with information of the current study; three of these organisations registered their interest. The sample of participants was obtained via a purposive sampling method, and participants were permitted to participate only if they met the following inclusion criteria: (i) completion of their training as per the guidance highlighted within NAAN, and thus work as a 'professional' AA within a designated scheme, and (ii) a minimum of three callouts to ensure an appropriate level of experience. The sample consisted of 14 participants (seven male and seven female), with a mean age of 60.2 years. The mean length of reported service was 3.28 years, and participation covered a large geographical area of England and Wales.

Materials

A semi-structured interview schedule was developed to capture the understanding and experiences of the AA role. Comprising open and probing questions to encourage long and detailed responses (King & Hugh-Jones, 2019), the interview schedule contained nine questions overall. These were based on gaps in the literature relating to the AAs' lived experiences; example questions included: 'Tell me about your role as an AA, and 'AAs are required to intervene during the suspect interview or on other occasions as part of their role. Explain a time when you had to do this.' The structure of these question types is typically favoured in Interpretative Phenomenological Analysis (IPA).

Procedure

Once a participant had registered their expression of interest, they were emailed an information sheet and consent form to read, complete, and return. The semi-structured interview was scheduled upon receiving the completed consent form, and these were conducted by telephone given the geographical spread of the participants. Each semi-structured interview was audio recorded on an iPad. At the beginning of each interview, the participant was encouraged to provide a pseudonym to ensure anonymity. The participant was then asked each question on the interview schedule and was encouraged to provide as much detail as possible. Once the semi-structured interview had finished, each participant was thanked for their time and provided with a debrief sheet. The interviews were then transcribed verbatim and analysed.

Design

In order to obtain rich and in-depth data, a qualitative design was utilised. IPA was adopted given the influence of phenomenology and hermeneutics – the former focusing on understanding the human experience and the latter trying to interpret the human experience (Shaw, 2019). Thus, the focus was to understand the AAs' experience of their role and to make interpretations of those experiences.

Data Analysis

Once all interviews were transcribed verbatim, IPA was conducted to each interview one at a time. This involved initially becoming familiar with the data by listening to the audio recording and re-reading the interview transcript. Initial themes were then identified in order to try and understand the participants' experiences (Shaw, 2019). This was achieved following two stages – first, descriptive summaries were recorded (phenomenological coding), and second, initial interpretations of the summaries were identified (interpretative coding). Exploring connections and commonly occurring concepts allowed for the data to be reduced further through the clustering of initial themes. The final superordinate and subordinate themes were then derived from the clusters. These were supported by identifying appropriate extracts from the interviews, thus representing the core concepts of the participants' experience.

Results

The analyses resulted in two superordinate and six subordinate themes emerging from the data (see Table 4.2). A brief summary is provided below but see Farrugia (submitted) for a full description.

1. Personal construction and experience of the Appropriate Adult role

1.1 UNDERSTANDING OF THE DYNAMIC NATURE OF THE APPROPRIATE ADULT ROLE

Predominately, participants described their role as supporting the vulnerable suspect in custody. However, there was some disparity in the views with some participants indicating that they are there to assist the police and others confirming that they do not have a working relationship with the police. Others suggested that their AA colleagues misunderstood their role: "We're there to do a job, and erm I think sometimes you have great voluntary people, but you also have voluntary people who aren't really aware of what

Table 4.2 Table of superordinate and subordinate themes

Superordinate Theme	Subordinate Theme
1. Personal construction and experience of the Appropriate Adult role	1.1 Understanding of the dynamic nature of the Appropriate Adult role
	1.2 Lived experience
	1.3 Regional and organisational differences
2. External construction and understanding of the Appropriate Adult role	2.1 Vulnerable suspects' understanding of the Appropriate Adult role
	2.2 Custody staffs' understanding and value of the Appropriate Adult role
	2.3 Hierarchy of roles

Source: Farrugia (submitted).

the actual full responsibility of the role is" (participant Elizabeth). This is demonstrated further when some participants claimed that their role is to be a friend to the vulnerable suspect in custody. Participants also alluded to the dynamic nature of their role with some making reference to assisting more than one vulnerable suspect at a time. Most participants reported the types of vulnerabilities and cases that they assist with, "...from affray to murder" (participant Elizabeth), and the types of working environments, such as the Department of Work and Pensions.

1.2 LIVED EXPERIENCE

Mixed experiences were reported by participants when working in custody. Participants were keen to express how they explain their role to the vulnerable suspect; "...the first thing we say to them is look, we're not the police. So...we're not siding with the police" (participant Patrick). Although some participants referred to positive experiences when working in custody, participants reported a substantial number of negative experiences. These related to the enactment of their role such as asking for custody processes to be repeated in front of them, the insistence of legal representation, and to intervening during the interview; "...there have been times when I've been called out of the interview and spoken to severely by the officer who says I shouldn't be intervening..." (participant Chloe). Such negative experiences were not limited to police officers but when working with solicitors and assisting other organisations. Consequently, some participants reported the impact that such negative experiences can have on the enactment of their role; this included not intervening any further during the interview in order to try and maintain the working relationship with the police officer. Thus, those that experience conflicts with other professionals in custody appear to alter their subsequent behaviour as a response.

1.3 REGIONAL AND ORGANISATIONAL DIFFERENCES

Some participants reported working across several different police force areas and identified a variability in the way in which they were treated. For example, one participant reported an instance of institutionalised racism:

> erm so I've had erm Appropriate Adults that are black erm... and they tried to arrest him and there is more times than

I count...but they've tried to put him back in the cell because they've assumed as he's sat in custody, that he's the actual detainee rather than the Appropriate Adult.

(participant Chloe)

Participants also reported differences in their treatment across different organisations with some participants making comparisons between the different settings in which they have worked:

so yeah, the RSPCA erm definitely want you there erm, erm when you're doing erm working with erm, erm social services erm with illegal immigrants yeah they, they like you to help them when they're doing age assessments etc., erm the police know you have to be there as opposed to them wanting you there I think.

(participant James)

2. External construction and understanding of the Appropriate Adult role

2.1 VULNERABLE SUSPECTS' UNDERSTANDING OF THE APPROPRIATE ADULT ROLE

Participants reported a commonly occurring misperception regarding how vulnerable suspects understood their role; despite the participants informing the vulnerable suspects of their role, participants reported that vulnerable suspects do not believe that they require an AA *and* a solicitor; "...I think if they...there's a- an Appropriate Adult there they feel erm they don't need to have erm a lawyer" (participant Tommy). Other participants highlighted that even when a vulnerable suspect does understand the difference between an AA and a solicitor, they still assume the AA to have more knowledge and power than their role allows. As such, it is apparent that the vulnerable suspects' understanding of the AA role often becomes confused with that of the solicitor even when AAs try to explain the difference.

2.2 CUSTODY STAFF'S UNDERSTANDING AND VALUE OF THE APPROPRIATE ADULT ROLE

Participants reported mixed levels of professional's understanding regarding their role as an AA. Some reported that there was very little understanding, whilst others believed that their role is well understood. Regardless, all participants identified that the value of the AA is procedural; that is, whilst the police may not want the AA present, they require them to be able to conduct their investigations accordingly:

> they do value our role because they can't do their job without it, if they want to erm interview and they haven't had an Appropriate Adult and they haven't followed the guidelines, then they've lost their case, cause the case they have to do it properly.
>
> (participant Slippers)

Participants also discussed what they believe to be the solicitor's perception of the AA role; such perceptions were mixed, with some positive and some negative. One participant reported:

> solicitors are very variable. Some of them- some of them don't want you there. Some of them are like you're not...you-re, you're there because you have to be there, but don't say anything, don't do anything, and certainly don't- don't er get into a conversation with- with my client.
>
> (participant Neil)

As such, it appears that professionals working within custody have variable levels of understanding and value of the AA role, with a particular emphasis on procedural value.

2.3 HIERARCHY OF ROLES

Many participants alluded to a hierarchical order of roles when working in custody. Some participants reflected upon a positive and equal working relationship that resulted in trust and being part of the police group; "and er I've found that very reassuring because they- they've included you in their conversations" (participant Veronica). Others suggest a more negative viewpoint, indicating that there is a hierarchy unless you are part of the 'in-group.' This was further evidenced when participants raised concerns regarding their perceptions of hierarchy for the more recently qualified AA. The perception of a hierarchy was not limited to police officers but also to solicitors working in custody:

erm I have more difficulty actually, with legal representative than anybody else that I work I think in this job. Erm er… some of them can be quite high handed and sort of I can't imagine why you're here, you know.

(participant Donna)

Theoretical Understanding

The findings from Farrugia (submitted) are one of the first studies that explore how AAs understand and perceive their role. Although many participants identified their role in line with the PACE (1984) and Code C (2018), some participants demonstrated some confusion when defining their role. Such ambiguity was also seen in how others appear to understand the role of the AA. Vulnerable suspects, for example, often assumed an overlap with that of the legal advisor. Furthermore, other professionals working in custody did not demonstrate a full understanding of the AA role, although it should be noted that these findings also suggest that the levels of understanding are variable based on region and organisation. As such, Farrugia's (submitted) findings reflect previous research that suggests that the AA role is a complex, demanding, and confusing one (Bartlett & Sandland, 2003; Cummins, 2011) and is open to interpretation (HMIC, 2015).

Farrugia (submitted) also reported that participants experienced a mix of positive and negative experiences, with a particular focus on the latter. Although the participants in her sample highlighted that police value their role from a procedural perspective, they also reported conflicts with all professionals working in custody and highlighted the impact that it would have on the subsequent enactment of their role. This included reducing the number of times they would intervene. This is concerning given that research has documented the passive nature of some AAs (e.g., Farrugia & Gabbert, 2019). However, this is not surprising given the conflict that AAs reportedly face (Farrugia, submitted).

Social Identity Theory (Tajfel & Turner, 1979) can provide some theoretical understanding to such group dynamics. This theory suggests that when individuals categorise themselves as belonging to or being part of an in-group, such individuals will make significant concessions, such as avoiding conflicts, to remain in their in-group. This is because individuals in the in-groups share common characteristics and distinguish themselves from out-groups. Unsurprisingly, individuals tend to view their in-groups more favourably than their out-groups. Furthermore, the way a social structure or hierarchy is enforced by those in authority can impact upon the relationships between groups with different statuses (Kreindler et al., 2012). Thus, within the context of AAs working in custody, this theory suggests that AAs may become passive to remain in their in-groups with the police and/or to avoid further conflict with those that they are working with. This may be exacerbated depending on which region and on which organisation they are working with.

Summary

Custody is a stressful environment and places those with vulnerabilities at an increased risk; research has documented how confusing such suspects can find the custodial process, particularly the investigative interview. As such, ensuring that vulnerable suspects are afforded the appropriate safeguards is vital. The AA role is defined in the PACE (1984), Code C (2018). However, despite its implementation, little psychological research has focused on the effect that the AA can have. It has been suggested that the AA remains passive in their role and that interventions are few and far between. This is supported by much more recent research; Farrugia and Gabbert (2019) found that AAs were much more likely to miss a reasonable opportunity to intervene than they were to intervene overall. However, they reported that when AAs do intervene, it is more likely to be an appropriate intervention rather than an inappropriate one.

Although several studies have reported the passivity of the AA, little research (if any) has focused on how the AA understands and experiences their role. Farrugia (submitted) conducted qualitative interviews with 14 professionally trained AAs and found there was some confusion regarding how they understood their role and how their role was understood by others, as well as the impact of conflict with other professionals on AAs performing their role. Underpinned by Social Identity Theory (Tajfel & Turner, 1979), this provides some understanding as to why AAs may become passive in their role; if AAs are faced with regular conflict when performing their role, they may be less likely to intervene to avoid further conflict. However, this raises several implications for practice; if AAs remain passive, then the risk of false confessions and miscarriages of justice increases as vulnerable suspects may provide misleading or inaccurate information during their interviews. Professionals may be less likely to engage with AA services given the lack of value they may perceive the AA to have. There remain high numbers of vulnerable individuals entering custody, and so it is essential that they are afforded the appropriate safeguards and that such safeguards are able to enact their role to their full potential.

Key Learning Points

- Suspects with mental health conditions and disorders are at a heightened risk of falsely confessing to crimes; thus, it is important that they are afforded the appropriate safeguards.
- The role of the AA has received little psychological attention since its implementation as per PACE (1984) and Code C (2018).
- The mainstream of research tends to focus on the implementation rates of the AA, or the availability of services.
- Recent research has documented that AA tend to be quite passive in their role, rather than actively intervening when required.
- Little research has focused on how AAs understand and experience their role.
- Farrugia (submitted) highlights how AA may be less likely to intervene should they face conflict, based on the theoretical understanding of Social Identity Theory.
- Further understanding and training is required for those professionals who work alongside the AA to ensure a collaborative approach that enables effective participation from all those involved in the assistance of a vulnerable suspect.
- Vulnerable suspects must be afforded the appropriate safeguards that can fully enact their role.

References

Bartlett, P. & Sandland, R. (2003). *Mental Health Law Policy and Practice.* Oxford: Oxford University Press.

Bath, C. (2014). *NAAN Briefing: Liaison and diversion and the provision of appropriate adults for mentally vulnerable adults.* London: National Appropriate Adult Network.

Chariot, P., Lepresle, A., Lefevre, T., Boraud, C., Barthes, A., & Tedlaouti, M. (2014). Alcohol and substance screening and brief intervention for detainees kept in police custody: A feasibility study. *Drug and Alcohol Dependence, 134,* 235–241.

Cummins, I. (2007). Boats against the current: Vulnerable adults in police custody. *The Journal of Adult Protection, 9*(1), 15–24.

Cummins, I. (2011). "The other side of silence": The role of the appropriate adult post Bradley. *Ethics and Social Welfare, 5*(3), 306–312.

Evans, R. (1993). *The conduct of police interviews with young people.* Royal Commission on Criminal Justice Research Study No.8. London: HMSO.

Farrugia, L. (submitted). The appropriate adult: Their perspective. *Submitted to Policing.*

Farrugia. L. & Gabbert, F. (2019). The appropriate adult: What they do and what they should do in police interviews with mentally disordered suspects. *Criminal Behaviour and Mental Health, 29*(3), 134–141.

Gudjonsson, G. (2018). *The psychology of false confessions: Forty years of science and practice.* West Sussex: John Wiley & Sons Ltd.

Heide, S. & Chan, T. (2016). Deaths in police custody. *Journal of Forensic and Legal Medicine, 57,* 109–114.

HM Inspectorate of Constabulary. (2015). *The welfare of vulnerable people in custody.* London: HMIC.

Home Office. (1984). *Police and Criminal Evidence Act (1984) and Codes of Practice (2018).* London: Home Office.

Hyun, E., Hahn, L., & McConnell, D. (2014). Experiences of people with learning disabilities in the Criminal Justice System. *British Journal of Learning Disabilities, 42,* 308–314.

Jessiman, T. & Cameron, A. (2017). The role of the Appropriate Adult in supporting vulnerable adults in custody: Comparing the perspectives of service users and service providers. *British Journal of Learning Disabilities, 45,* 246–252.

King, N. & Hugh-Jones, S. (2019). The interview in qualitative research. In C. Sullivan & M. Forrester (Eds.), *Doing qualitative research in psychology: A practical guide* (pp. 121–144). London: Sage.

Kreindler, S., Dowd, D., Star, N., & Gottschalk, T. (2012). Silos and social identity: The social identity approach as a framework for understanding and overcoming divisions in healthcare. *Milbank Q, 90,* 347–374.

Leahy-Harland, S. (2013). *Police interviewing of serious crime suspects.* (Unpublished doctoral dissertation). Leicester: University of Leicester.

McKinnon, I. & Grubin, D. (2010). Health screening in police custody. *Journal of Forensic and Legal Medicine, 17,* 209–212.

Medford, S., Gudjonsson, G., & Pearse, J. (2003). The efficacy of the appropriate adult safeguard during police interviewing. *Legal and Criminological Psychology, 8*(2), 253–266.

Miller, R. (2015). An exploration of mental health triage and support in the criminal justice system: Attitudes and experiences of professionals supporting people with mental health needs. (Unpublished doctoral dissertation).

Nemitz, T. & Bean, P. (2001). Protecting the rights of the MD in police stations: The use of the Appropriate Adult in England and Wales. *International Journal of Law and Psychiatry, 24,* 595–605.

Newburn, T. (2013). *Criminology*. Abingdon: Routledge.

Pierpoint, H. (2000). How appropriate are volunteers as "Appropriate Adults" for young suspects? *Journal of Social Welfare and Family Law, 22*, 383–400.

Pierpoint, H. (2001). The performance of volunteer appropriate adults: A survey of call outs. *Howard Journal of Criminal Justice, 40*(3), 255–271.

Pierpoint, H. (2006). Reconstructing the role of the Appropriate Adult in England and Wales. *Criminology and Criminal Justice, 6*, 219–237.

Pierpoint, H. (2011). Extending and professionalising the role of the Appropriate Adult. *Journal of Social Welfare and Family Law, 33*(2), 139–155.

Shaw, R. (2019). Interpretative phenomenological analysis. In C. Sullivan & M. Forrester (Eds.), *Doing qualitative research in psychology. A practical guide* (pp. 185–208). London: Sage.

Soukara, S. (2004). *Investigating interviewing of suspects: Piecing together the picture.* (Unpublished doctoral dissertation). Portsmouth: University of Portsmouth.

Tajfel, H. & Turner, J. (1979). An integrative theory of intergroup conflict. In G. Austin & S. Worchel (Eds.), *The social psychology of intergroup relations* (pp. 33–47). Monterey, CA: Brooks-Cole.

5 The Vulnerable Suspect

The Impact on the Investigative Interview

Given the over-representation of vulnerable suspects in the criminal justice system (CJS; Sirdifield & Brooker, 2012), those involved in conducting investigative interviews with suspects that have mental health conditions and disorders need to have an understanding of how such suspects are likely to engage and communicate during such a vital stage. This is particularly important as a large body of research has documented the fallibility of memory and the nature of the retrieval process as easily influenced by police questioning and police behaviour (Baddeley et al., 2009). Furthermore, suspects with mental health conditions and disorders do not respond well to traditional methods of policing (Gudjonsson, 2018), and their needs are not well understood (Baksheev et al., 2010). Interviewers' questions, therefore, need to be matched to the abilities of those that they are interviewing (Powell, 2002). However, interviewing a vulnerable suspect is not an easy task (Herrington & Roberts, 2012). The presentation of a vulnerable suspect may be dependent upon their specific mental health condition or disorder.

Mood Disorders

Mood disorder is a general term used to describe all types of depression and bipolar disorders, and it is generally characterised by behavioural, emotional, and cognitive symptoms. These can include marked weight loss or gain, insomnia, fatigue, feelings of guilt or worthlessness, concentration difficulties, emotion dysregulation, and negative affect (Gotlib & Joorman, 2010). Depression is perhaps one of the most common mood disorders with approximately one in six adults experiencing at least one episode in their lifetime (Office for National Statistics, 2021). Given the high recurrence rate of this mood disorder (Boland & Keller, 2009), it is extremely likely that those with depression may come into contact with

DOI: 10.4324/9781003161028-5

custody. Indeed, depression has been reported by approximately half of all prisoners (Burki, 2017). As such, it is important to understand the specific characteristics of this type of mood disorder and how they may impact upon the investigative interview.

One important consideration is how individuals with depression attend to information presented to them or asked of them. Research has documented that those with depression tend to attend to personal concerns and other thoughts that are irrelevant to the task (Ellis & Ashbrook, 1988), thus impacting upon control of attention and subsequent level of engagement and recall. For example, in early research, Hertel (1998) found deficits in recall between students with mood disorders who were required to wait in an unconstrained situation without being given specific instructions regarding what to do during the waiting period, and those students with mood disorders who were given specific instructions. Following a series of studies, Hertel and colleagues found that depression-related impairments are found primarily in free recall tasks (Hertel, 1998; Hertel & Rude, 1991). Their findings suggest that individuals with depression may have the ability to perform at the same level as individuals without any mental health conditions or disorders when they are provided with structured situations or instructions (Hertel, 2004), as the opportunity to ruminate is eliminated. That is, when attention is well controlled by the demands of the task, and thus opportunities for rumination are reduced, the depressive deficits relating to attention and recall are reduced (Hertel, 2004).

Control of attention and recall can impact upon memory. Overall, there is a strong evidence base for biased memory processes in individuals that have depression (Mathews & MacLeod, 2005). Generally, such vulnerable individuals tend to have a higher recall and encoding of negative rather than positive material (Mathews & MacLeod, 2005). In addition, an attentional bias towards emotional stimuli, known as a cognitive bias, congruent with their mood has been found in individuals with depression (Beck, 1976, 1987; Blaney, 1986; Lemogne et al., 2006). Given that individuals with depression selectively attend to emotional cues (Beevers et al., 2009) and that ambiguous information is generally interpreted in a negative manner (Rude et al., 2002), individuals with depression have a negative bias in all types of their information processing (Beevers & Carver, 2003).

This has implications for the investigative interview. At the start of this process, the suspect should be asked, usually by an open question, for a 'free recall' of their alleged involvement in the reported crime. Given that depression-related impairments are primarily found in these types of tasks (Hertel, 1998; Hertel & Rude, 1991), it is likely that suspects with depression may find this difficult to complete; the wide nature of the open question used to request the free recall may allow for opportunities of rumination and may not provide enough structured instructions to control the attention of the suspect with depression. Furthermore, the free recall requested at the start of the investigative interview draws upon the episodic memory. This is an explicit memory task, and according to Beck's Schema Model (Beck, 1976) and Bowers Spreading Activation theory (Bower, 1981), mood congruent cognitive biases are evident in a wide range of cognitive processes, including explicit memory tasks such as the free recall within an investigative interview. Thus, in addition to the free recall task allowing for those with depression to ruminate given the unstructured nature of such an instruction, suspects with depressions may be at a heightened risk of falsely implicating themselves given the tendency to selectively attend to emotional cues, particularly if the alleged offence is distressing or emotional.

Anxiety

Anxiety has been defined by scholars as a response to prolonged and unpredictable threat, of which the response encompasses physiological, affective, and cognitive changes (Davis et al., 2010). The *Diagnostic and Statistical Manual 5* (*DSM-5*; American Psychiatric Association [APA], 2013) outlines specific criteria to help with the diagnosis of an anxiety disorder. These include the presence of excessive anxiety and worry more often than not for a period of at least six months, the worry that is experienced refers to a variety of events or activities and is difficult to control, and the anxiety and worry experienced is accompanied by at least three other physical or cognitive symptoms. These include feeling on edge or restless, feeling fatigued, impaired concentration and/ or irritability, muscle soreness, and difficulty sleeping. Anxiety disorders are a worldwide mental health concern (Robinson et al., 2013) and this is echoed within the UK offender population; indeed, research has documented that approximately 36% of offenders have an anxiety disorder (Tyler et al., 2019).

Individuals with this condition experience impaired cognitive processes relating to intrusive thoughts and emotions, and dysregulated attention mechanisms including impaired concentration (Eysenck et al., 2007). These symptoms have been linked to an attentional bias for threat; individuals with an anxiety disorder show a predisposition to detect and process threat-related information, which subsequently interferes with performance in other attentional tasks (Bar-Haim et al., 2007; Cisler

& Koster, 2010; Macleod & Mathews, 2012). Cognitive models that attempt to explain anxiety have been critical in highlighting how such attentional biases operate at an early stage of information processing. Furthermore, there is substantial evidence that suggests such biases are not inflexible but are strongly influenced by environmental stressors (Wald et al., 2013). As such, if an individual with an anxiety disorder experiences environmental stressors when in custody, then this suggests that attentional biases will be exacerbated. Furthermore, the cognitive models that explain anxiety highlight that the anxiety experienced by an individual draws upon neural resources that are critical to memory subsequently resulting in decreased accuracy and recall.

Episodic and working memory are crucial cognitive processes when one considers what happens in an investigative interview. Seeking a free recall at the start of the interview draws upon the episodic memory of an individual. However, individuals with an anxiety disorder have been shown to exhibit impairments in episodic memory (Airaksinen et al., 2005). Furthermore, working memory is drawn upon when one considers how information is held in the memory and utilised to execute cognitive tasks, such as responding to questions. Working memory is impaired in individuals with an anxiety disorder (Lindstrom & Bohlin, 2012). This is line with processing efficiency theory (Eysenck & Calvo, 1992) that highlights that anxious worry reduces working memory capacity and increases the necessary effort needed to perform the task. This subsequently increases the individuals' reaction time. In addition, some research has indicated that the impact of anxiety on verbal working memory, the ability to retain information and then use it for learning or reasoning (such as responding to a question), is dependent upon the cognitive load (Vytal et al., 2012, 2013).

Schizophrenia

Schizophrenia is characterised by delusions, hallucinations, disorganised speech, disorganised or catatonic behaviour, and negative symptoms. According to the *DSM-5* (APA, 2013), two of these symptoms are required and at least one of the symptoms must be delusions, hallucinations, or disorganised speech. It is estimated that approximately 1 in 100 individuals will experience at least one episode of schizophrenia in their lifetime (Royal College of Psychiatrists, 2017) and that approximately 8% of the prison population have a diagnosis (Durcan, 2021). As such, this has implications for those with schizophrenia entering the CJS and the impact on the investigative interview.

Generally, research has consistently documented cognitive impairments as core features of schizophrenia (Bora et al., 2010; Guo et al., 2019). These relate specifically to impairments in attention, processing speed, working memory, and executive functions. However, perhaps one of the biggest impairments in those with schizophrenia relate to the episodic memory and working memory. Research has documented prominent prefrontal deficits in individuals with schizophrenia during both encoding and retrieval of episodic memory tasks (Ragland et al., 2009), and such deficits are specific to tasks that involve high cognitive demands (Guo et al., 2019). Furthermore, impairments in working memory in individuals with schizophrenia are characterised by reduced accuracy and the need for longer response time in recall (Fusar-Poli et al., 2012; White et al., 2010).

Episodic memory is important in the investigative interview, particularly with a suspect; being able to recall previous experiences or events is necessary should one be implicated in a crime. However, research exploring cognitive impairments in individuals with schizophrenia has reported that episodic memory is impaired, especially if the task is particularly cognitively demanding. This also impacts upon working memory. Working memory refers to a temporary storage system that can be used to encode, rehearse, and manipulate information in mind (Jonides et al., 2008). Thus, if a task is cognitively demanding, the demands placed on cognitive resources, such as the working memory, mean that the processing of information is restricted (van Merrienboer & Sweller, 2010), consequently having implications for the processing and retrieval of information required by a suspect during an investigative interview. That is, during tasks that an individual finds cognitively demanding, the amount of mental effort required also increases (Kleider-Offutt et al., 2016). This may lead to an 'attentional bottleneck' where attending to one cognitively demanding task causes other cognitive processes to be neglected (Strayer & Drews, 2007). Thus, the attentional demands required to perform complex tasks may lead to errors or a reduction in performance (Engle & Kane, 2004). Vulnerable suspects with impairments in these areas may then provide inaccurate or misleading information that may falsely implicate themselves due to the impairments in their episodic and working memory and the cognitively demanding task that is an investigative interview.

However, research has also documented that such individuals can be assisted with their recall, despite the cognitive impairments associated with schizophrenia. The use of instructions has been found to be beneficial to those with schizophrenia (Guimond et al., 2017). For example, Aleman et al. (1999) found that patients with schizophrenia showed significantly better memory performance when retrieval cues were provided. When translated into the investigative interview, this seems to suggest that should a vulnerable suspect with schizophrenia be provided with specific questioning strategies, rather than those using only open questions, the impact of their deficits may be reduced.

General Vulnerabilities

Overgeneral Memory

In addition to the specific difficulties suspects with mental health conditions or disorders may experience during the investigative interview, there are general factors that can affect all vulnerable suspects. One of these is known as an overgeneral memory. This relates to the concept that vulnerable individuals recall generic memories or repeated events, rather than specific events or single episodes (Williams et al., 2007). This is particularly prevalent in individuals with depression and post-traumatic stress disorder (PTSD; Lemogne et al., 2006). Williams (1996) suggested that an overgeneral memory is an individual's way of emotion regulation. Williams explained that individuals attempt to minimise negative emotions attached to distressing memories by blocking access to details of those memories or by retrieving those memories in a less specific way. An overgeneral memory can result in the vulnerable suspect finding it difficult to recall specific events and in the correct order, difficulties in concentrating, and attending to questions asked of them (Kingdon & Turkington, 2005).

Suggestibility, Compliance, and Acquiescence

Vulnerable individuals, particularly those with mental health conditions and disorders, may be particularly prone to heightened levels of suggestibility, compliance, and acquiescence (Gudjonsson, 2010, 2018). Suggestibility is defined as "the extent to which, within a closed social interaction, people come to accept messages communicated during formal questioning, as a result of which their subsequent behavioural response is affected" (Gudjonsson & Clark, 1987, p.84), and can be measured by the Gudjonsson Suggestibility Scale (GSS; Gudjonsson, 1984, 1987). Gudjonsson suggests that suggestibility arises out of the way in which the individual interacts with others within the environment and is dependent upon the coping strategies employed by the individual. For example, during an investigative interview, the individual has to cognitively process the question and the context in which it is taking place. The process of coping with this involves the individual having to cope with uncertainty, interpersonal trust, and expectations. It is these three components that are essential prerequisites for suggestibility and that can be manipulated during the interview process. Literature has consistently found that suggestibility is influenced by cognitive factors such as intelligence, memory, and language (Bruck & Melnyk, 2004), as well as factors such as anxiety and self-esteem (Goodman et al., 2014). One particular factor of importance relates to exposure to adverse life events and the subsequent presence of mental health conditions or disorders, including anxiety and PTSD (Vagni et al., 2021). Research has documented that those who have experienced such adverse life events may be at particular risk of higher levels of suggestibility (Drake, 2014).

Compliance can be described as "the tendency of the individual to go along with propositions, requests, or instructions for some immediate instrumental gain" (Gudjonsson, 1992, p.137). This can be measured via the Gudjonsson Compliance Scale (GCS; Gudjonsson, 1997). Key components to compliant behaviour include an eagerness to please and an avoidance of conflict, particularly with those perceived to be an authority figure. Compliance has been explored in relation to individuals' motivation to engage with offending behaviour (Gudjonsson & Sigurdsson, 2004), as well as falsely confessing to a crime (Gudjonsson et al., 2007). Other research has identified a link between intelligence and IQ and individuals with attention deficit hyperactivity disorder (ADHD); researchers exploring the latter have found that inattention and hyperactivity/impulsivity were most correlated with compliance (Gudjonsson & Sigurdsson, 2010).

Early scholars identified acquiescence as the tendency to agree with or say yes to statements or questions regardless of their content (Block, 1965). Also known as "yea-saying" (Finlay & Lyons, 2002), or "the tendency of the person to answer questions affirmatively irrespective of content" (Gudjonsson, 1990), early research in an academic context that investigated true-false tests found that students tended to answer "true" when in doubt (Cronbach, 1950). Other early research investigating item reversals found a systematic bias in response to yes/no questions (Sigelman et al., 1982; Sigelman & Budd, 1986), and a link to IQ scores (Gudjonsson, 1990), although contradictory findings have also been reported (Matikka & Vesala, 1997). Acquiescence is also reported to occur when the answer to the question is not known (Cronback, 1950), when questions are ambiguous to the individual (Ray, 1983), and when the individual has a lack of motivation or limited cognitive ability to consider the question (Knowles & Condon, 1999; Javeline, 1999). Some research has also found that acquiescence arises when the question structure is too lengthy or complex for the individual or grammatically too complex (Shaw & Budd, 1982). For example, individuals may respond to the topic of the question whilst not fully understanding the subtleties of its phrasing (Heal & Sigelman, 1995). Gudjonsson (1990) describes being acquiescent as involving three stages. The first is having the ability to listen to the question, which involves paying attention and interest. The second stage is understanding the question, which involves understanding the vocabulary, having general knowledge about the topic, and having overall comprehension. At this stage, if the individual does not understand the question, then uncertainty develops and the individual may then guess the answer, give the most plausible response, or indicate their uncertainty. Consequently, Gudjonsson (1990) suggests that acquiescence functions to reduce the apparent uncertainty and restore self-esteem. High levels of acquiescence have been found in individuals with mental health conditions and disorders (Clare & Gudjonsson, 1993; Perlman et al., 1994), with research reporting that those who acquiescence may not be fully aware of the consequences of their responses (Clare & Gudjonsson, 1995).

The Impact on the Investigative Interview: Literature Base

It is well established that conducting investigative interviews with suspects is an integral and crucial part of the evidence gathering process (Oxburgh & Ost, 2011; Williamson, 2006). However, there has been very little research conducted in exploring the investigative interview and the impact of various question types on vulnerable suspects, particularly those with mental health conditions and disorders. Of the research that has been conducted, the focus has been on the impact of intellectual disabilities and mental health conditions on the reliability of eyewitness accounts (Gudjonsson, 2010). Studies that have focused directly on the interview process have found some interesting results that cast doubt upon the appropriateness of open questions for all populations. For example, three independent studies have found that adults with intellectual disability report fewer correct details than those without an intellectual disability when asked open questions that invite a free narrative response (Bowles & Sharman, 2014; Perlman et al., 1994; Ternes & Yuille, 2008).

More recent research has explored the impact of question typology on individuals with an Autism Spectrum Condition (ASC) and has highlighted that such individuals have difficulties with their episodic memory, particularly on tasks requiring a free narrative account of experienced events (Crane et al., 2012). Subsequently, this vulnerable group typically recalls significantly less information and less accurate information about experienced events than those without an ASC (Maras & Bowler, 2010; Maras et al., 2012). However, when those with an ASC are provided with cued or directed recall, their performance is equivalent to that of control participants, that is those that do not have an ASC (Maras & Bowler, 2011; Maras et al., 2013).

There appears to be an emerging branch of research that casts doubt on the appropriateness of the use of open questions and free recall for vulnerable populations. Indeed, in recent research, police officers have cited that whilst open questions are best practice generally, police officers highlighted that they are not always suitable for suspects with mental health conditions or disorders. They explained that actually open questions can be too broad and that the use of specific questions can actually aid a vulnerable suspect's understanding (L. Oxburgh et al., 2016). However, there is very little research into the investigative interviewing of suspects with mental health conditions or disorders. This is concerning given the documented difficulties that these suspects may face. The work of Farrugia and Gabbert (2019) provides some insight into the interviewing of such vulnerable suspects.

Vulnerable Suspects in Police Interviews: Exploring Current Practice in England and Wales (Farrugia & Gabbert, 2019)

Aims

The aims of this study sought to examine current investigative interview practice in England and Wales with suspects that have mental health conditions and disorders, and to explore how these vulnerable suspects respond to procedures, questioning techniques, and the impact this has on investigation relevant information (IRI). The following research questions were addressed:

(i)   Do officers alter their interview style when interviewing suspects with and without a mental health condition or disorder?

(ii) Do suspects with and without a mental health condition or disorder respond differently to question types?

(iii) Do suspects with a mental health condition or disorder display more vulnerability, suggestibility, and compliance than suspects without a mental health condition and disorder?

Given the exploratory nature of the study, no hypotheses were generated.

Method

Ethical approval was gained from the Faculty of Humanities and Social Sciences at the University of Portsmouth. In addition, the researcher was vetted in order to obtain the data.

Sample

Five police forces in England and Wales provided a sample of police interviews that had been conducted with suspects with and without mental health conditions or disorders, who had been implicated in a serious offence. Interview data were obtained via a research contact in each police force. The interviews were included in the final sample only if the suspect provided an account and if the case was classified as closed. The final sample consisted of 66 interviews conducted with suspects with mental health conditions or disorders (n = 30) and suspects without (n = 36).

Materials

A coding framework and guide was developed based on current interview practice in England and Wales and relevant psychological research (e.g., G. Oxburgh et al., 2012). The coding framework consisted of nine sections that focused specifically on the "E," "A," and "C" of the PEACE model of interviewing and was designed to explore current interview practice:

(i)   Engage and explain: This focused on procedural areas that would be reasonably expected of an interviewer to complete; for example, explaining the process of the interview, the legal rights, and the caution.

(ii) Account, clarify, and challenge: This coded for question types based on current classifications (see Chapter 1), and interviewer and suspect characteristics such as the use of minimisation, maximisation, and repetitive questioning, and any instances of vulnerability relating to suggestibility, compliance, and acquiescence. The amount of IRI elicited from the suspect was also coded for (see G. Oxburgh et al., 2012 for a full description).

(iii) Closure: This focused on how the interviewer(s) concluded the interview, including management of tapes/discs, whether a summary was provided, and explanations of future processes.

Alongside the coding framework, a coding guide was developed to provide operational definitions for each aspect of the coding and to ensure that coding was consistent across all interview data.

Procedure

Each interview was read by the researcher before the coding framework was applied using the coding guide and the operational definitions. The coding of the data focused on each utterance of the interviewer(s) and the suspect. As the 'Engage and explain' and 'Closure' stage focused on procedural areas, these were coded for their presence or their absence during the interview. Such dichotomous coding also took place for the initial procedural aspects of the 'Account, clarify, and challenge' stage. For the rest of the coding, instances of each question type, amount of IRI, and interviewer(s) and suspect characteristics were recorded each time that they occurred. Given the difficulties in differentiating between suggestibility, compliance, and acquiescence outside of clinical practice, any instances of this were combined and recorded as suspect vulnerability.

Design

A between-within subjects design was utilised with two conditions: (i) suspects with mental health conditions and disorders and (ii) suspects without mental health conditions and disorders.

Data Analysis

Given the exploratory nature of the research, a number of statistical tests were run in accordance with the research questions. Prior to this, inter-rater reliability was assessed. A sample of the interview transcripts ($n = 13$; 20%) were double coded. Cohen's kappa, recommended for assessing inter-rater reliability for categorical variables, was applied to the dichotomous coding (Cohen, 1969). An almost perfect agreement was achieved between the two researchers' judgements with Cohen's kappa ranging from .87 to .91. Intraclass correlation was applied to the continuous variables (Hallgren, 2012). Inter-rater correlations were .86 to .98 for question types, .89 to .94 and .91 to .97 for interviewer and suspect characteristics, respectively, and .78 to .85 for IRI, indicating good to excellent reliability (Koo & Li, 2016).

Results

General Characteristics of the Interview Sample

The interviews included in this sample (n = 66) had been conducted in England and Wales between 2002 and 2015. Overall, the suspects were predominately male (n = 59), and the interviews tended to involve two interviewers (n = 61), with the first interviewer largely being male (n = 35) and the second interviewer largely being male too (n = 44). A Legal Advisor was present in the majority of all suspect interviews (n = 57) and an Appropriate Adult was present in the majority of interviews conducted with suspects with mental health conditions or disorders (n = 29) with a mental health nurse also present in a small number of these interviews (n = 2). The types of mental health conditions and disorders recorded in the interviews involving the vulnerable suspects included schizophrenia (n = 6), mood disorders (n = 3), psychosis (n = 2), dissociative identity disorder (n = 2), anxiety (n = 1), and personality disorder (n = 1). In half of the vulnerable sample, the suspect was recorded as having mental health issues, but this was unspecified on police records (n = 15). The type of crimes that the suspects were interviewed about included murder/attempted murder (n = 25), rape (n = 22), sexual assaults (n = 13), child internet offences (n = 5), and sex with a minor (n = 1). The vulnerable suspect group was significantly more likely to provide a full admission than suspects without any mental health conditions or disorders, $\chi^2(2)$ = 7.09, p = .03. Other characteristics for the interview sample are recorded in Table 5.1.

Table 5.1 Table of overall characteristics of interview sample (Farrugia & Gabbert, 2019)

Interview Characteristic	Type of Suspect Interview	
	Non-vulnerable Suspects	Vulnerable Suspects
Length of Interview	66.44 Minutes	103.2 Minutes
Number of Interviews Completed	2 Interviews	3 Interviews
Type of Admission:		
Full Admission	$N = 2$	$N = 9$
Partial Admission	$N = 9$	$N = 5$
No Admission	$N = 25$	$N = 16$

Procedural Aspects

Generally, interviewer(s) remained consistent in their approach between the two suspect groups in that there were no significant differences between large aspects of procedures relating to the 'Engage and explain' and the 'Closure' stages. Interestingly, suspects with mental health conditions and disorders were significantly more likely to be informed of the interview topics to be covered in their interview, $\chi^2(29) = 4.63$, $p = .03$, and were more likely to be informed that the police interview was an opportunity to provide their account, $\chi^2(29) = 4.75$, $p = .03$, when compared with suspects with no mental health conditions and disorders.

Eliciting Information

Question Type

The use of appropriate and inappropriate questions used in all suspect interviews was explored. A Mann–Whitney U test indicated that there were no significant differences in the overall number of appropriate questions asked between the two suspect groups, $U = 480.00$, $p = .44$, $N = 66$, nor in the overall number of inappropriate questions asked between the two suspect groups, $U = 469.00$, $p = .36$, $N = 66$. However, when analysis focused within groups, suspects with mental health conditions and disorders were asked significantly more inappropriate questions ($M = 2.70$, $SD = 1.09$) than appropriate questions ($M = 1.66$, $SD = 1.15$) during their police interviews, $t = 5.48$, $p < .01$. This was also reflected in interviews conducted with suspects with no mental health conditions and disorders; that is, they were asked significantly more inappropriate questions ($M = 2.44$, $SD = 1.21$) than appropriate questions ($M = 1.42$, $SD = .80$) during their police interviews, $t = 5.99$, $p < .01$.

Clarification of Question Types
The need for clarification was initially explored between the two suspect groups. A Mann–Whitney U Test indicated that overall, there were no significant differences in requests for questions to be clarified between suspects with mental health conditions and disorders (mean rank = 36.65) and suspects with no mental health conditions and disorders (mean rank = 30.88), $U = 445.50$, $p = .22$, $N = 66$. However, significant differences were found when examining the need for clarification on specific question types. For example, suspects with mental health conditions and disorders were significantly more likely to seek clarification to open questions (mean rank = 37.13) compared to suspects with no mental health conditions and disorders (mean rank = 30.47), $U = 431.00$, $p = .05$, $N = 66$. Furthermore, suspects with mental health conditions and disorders were more likely to seek clarification to encouragers/acknowledgement-style questions (mean rank = 35.30) compared to suspects with no mental health conditions and disorders, $U = 486.00$, $p = .05$, $N = 66$. This was also the case with forced choice questions; suspects with mental health conditions and disorders were significantly more likely to seek clarification (mean rank = 35.30) than suspects with no mental health conditions and disorders (mean rank = 32.00), $U = 486.00$, $p = .05$, $N = 66$.

Investigation Relevant Information

The amount of IRI obtained from both suspect groups was explored to examine which, if any, question type elicited the most information. Overall, there were no significant differences found in the amount of IRI provided between suspects with mental health conditions and disorders ($M = 5.03$, $SD = 2.03$) and those without mental health conditions and disorders ($M = 5.79$, $SD = 2.18$), $t = 1.44$, $p = .15$. However, analyses that focused specifically on question type and the amount of IRI found some significant differences. Suspects with no mental health conditions and disorders provided a significantly higher amount of IRI in response to multiple questions ($M = .45$, $SD = .43$) when compared to suspects with mental health conditions and disorders ($M = .25$, $SD = .25$), $t = 2.20$, $p = .03$. Furthermore, when examining the impact of open v closed questions on the level of IRI, suspects with mental health conditions and disorders provided significantly more IRI to closed questions ($M = .81$, $SD = .55$) than open questions ($M = .02$, $SD = .02$), $t = 8.05$, $p < .001$. This was also the case for suspects with no mental health conditions and disorders; that is, this suspect group provided significantly more IRI to closed questions ($M = .91$, $SD = .71$) than to open questions ($M = .51$, $SD = .81$), $t = 2.14$, $p = .04$.

Suspect Vulnerability

Interviewer Behaviours
Analyses focusing on interviewer behaviours produced some interesting findings. Interviewers were significantly more likely to alter their language to suit the abilities and understanding of suspects with mental health conditions and disorders ($M = 2.83$, $SD = 2.73$) when compared to suspects with no mental health conditions and disorders ($M = 1.53$, $SD = 1.36$), $t = 2.52$, $p = .01$. However, interviewers were significantly more likely to use poor interview techniques such as minimisation during interviews with suspects with mental health conditions and disorders ($M = .01$, $SD = .01$) than with the non-vulnerable suspects ($M = <.001$, $SD < .001$), $t = 1.81$, $p = .05$.

Suspect Behaviours

Analysis indicated that suspects with mental health conditions and disorders demonstrated significantly higher levels of vulnerability ($M = .02$, $SD = .04$) than suspects with no mental health conditions and disorders ($M = .003$, $SD = .01$), $t = 2.16$, $p = .04$.

Summary

The aim of any investigative interview is to obtain accurate and reliable information (G. Oxburgh et al., 2010). This is also true in interviews conducted with suspects with mental health conditions and disorders.

However, these types of suspects do not respond well to traditional policing methods. Depending on the type of mental health condition or disorder, the vulnerable suspect may present with deficits in processing and memory and, as such, are subsequently at a heightened risk of falsely implicating themselves during the police interview (Gudjonsson, 2018). Furthermore, research has consistently documented the increasing levels of suggestibility, compliance, and acquiescence suspects with mental health conditions and disorders may present with. This places them at a significant disadvantage within the CJS, and thus it is imperative that those conducting the investigative interviews with this suspect group are equipped to do so (Herrington & Roberts, 2012).

The research base concerning the investigative interviewing of suspects with mental health conditions and disorders is scarce. The work of Farrugia and Gabbert (2019) aimed to examine current interview practice with this suspect group. Their main findings suggested that current best practice interviewing methods, such as the use of open questions, were not being entirely adhered to (consistent with other findings – see Snook and Keating [2010]) and may not be entirely suitable for suspects with mental health conditions and disorders in terms of their level of understanding and the amount of IRI elicited. Their results also highlighted that such vulnerable suspects were subjected to significantly increased levels of minimisation when compared to the non-vulnerable suspect sample; such interview techniques imply leniency and increase the rate of false confessions (Narchet et al., 2011). More positive findings suggested that interviewers changed their language to suit the abilities of the vulnerable suspect. The work of Farrugia and Gabbert (2019) is one of the first in examining overall how suspects with mental health conditions and disorders cope during the investigative interview and raises important implications for the interviewing of this vulnerable suspect group; is best practice really best practice?

Key Learning Points

- Vulnerable suspects are over-represented in the CJS and do not respond well to traditional methods of policing.
- Research has documented that those with depression have impairments relating to free recall tasks and episodic memory.
- Individuals with an anxiety disorder have impairments in episodic and working memory.

- Impairments in episodic memory have also been found in individuals with schizophrenia – such deficits are specific to tasks requiring high cognitive load.

- Individuals with mental health conditions and disorders may also experience general vulnerabilities, such as an overgeneral memory, heightened levels of suggestibility, compliance, and acquiescence. This places them at a disadvantage when they enter the CJS.

- Whilst research advocates for the use of best practice interviewing methods such as the use of open questions, there is an emerging branch of research that casts doubt on the appropriateness of open questions and the free recall technique for vulnerable populations.

- Farrugia and Gabbert's (2019) research found that the use of open questions may not be suitable for suspects with mental health conditions and disorders.

- Further work is required to examine this in more detail; the interviewer must be able to ask questions that are matched to the abilities of the vulnerable suspect.

References

Airaksinen, E., Larsson, M., & Forsell, Y. (2005). Neuropsychological functions in anxiety disorders in population-based samples: Evidence of episodic memory dysfunction. *Journal of Psychiatric Research, 39*, 207–214.

Aleman, A., Hijman, R., de Haan, E., & Kahn, R. (1999). Memory impairment in schizophrenia: A meta-analysis. *American Journal of Psychiatry, 156*(9), 1358–1366.

American Psychiatric Association. (2013). *Diagnostic and statistical manual of mental disorders* (5th ed.). Arlington, VA: American Psychiatric Association.

Baddeley, A., Eysenck, M., & Anderson, M. (2009). *Memory.* Sussex: Psychology Press.

Baksheev, G., Thomas, S., & Ogloff, J. (2010). Psychiatric disorders and unmet needs in Australian police cells. *Australian and New Zealand Journal of Psychiatry, 44*, 1043–1051.

Bar-Haim, Y., Lamy, D., Pergamin, L., Bakermans-Kranenburg, M., & van Ijzendoorn, M. (2007). Threat-related attentional bias in anxious and nonanxious individuals: A meta-analytic study. *Psychological Bulletin, 133*, 1–24.

Beck, A. (1976). *Cognitive therapy and the emotional disorders.* Oxford: International Universities Press.

Beck, A. (1987). Cognitive models of depression. *Journal of Cognitive Psychotherapy, 1*, 5–37.

Beevers, C. & Carver, C. (2003). Attentional bias and mood persistence as prospective predictors of dysphoria. *Cognitive Therapy and Research, 27*, 619–637.

Beevers, C., Wells, T., Ellis, A., & McGeary, J. (2009). Association of the serotonin transporter gene promotor region (5-HTTLPR) polymorphism with biased attention for emotional stimuli. *Journal of Abnormal Psychology, 118*(3), 670–681.

Blaney, P. (1986). Affect and memory: A review. *Psychological Bulletin, 99*, 229–246.

Block, J. (1965). *The challenge of response sets: Unconfounding meaning, acquiescence, and social desirability in the MMPI.* New York: Appleton Century-Crofts.

Boland, R. & Keller, M. (2009). Course and outcome of depression. In I. Gotlib & C. Hammen (Eds.), *Handbook of depression* (pp. 23–43). New York: Guildford.

Bora, E., Yucel, M., & Pantelis, C. (2010). Cognitive impairment in schizophrenia and affective psychoses: Implications for DSM-V criteria and beyond. *Schizophrenia Bulletin, 36*(1), 36–42.

Bower, G. (1981). Mood and memory. *American Psychologist, 36*, 129–148.

Bowles, P. & Sharman, S. (2014). A review of the impact of different types of leading interview questions on child and adult witnesses with intellectual disabilities. *Psychiatry, Psychology and Law, 21*(2), 205–217.

Bruck, M. & Melnyk, L. (2004). Individual differences in children's suggestibility: A review and synthesis. *Applied Cognitive Psychology, 18*, 947–996.

Burki, T. (2017). Crisis in UK prison mental health. *The Lancet Psychiatry, 4*(12), 904.

Cisler, J. & Koster, E. (2010). Mechanisms of attentional biases towards threat in the anxiety disorders: An integrative review. *Clinical Psychology Review, 30*(2), 203–216.

Clare, I. & Gudjonsson, G. (1993). Interrogative suggestibility, confabulation, and acquiescence in people with mild learning disabilities (mental handicap): Implications for reliability during police interrogations. *British Journal of Clinical Psychology, 32*, 295–301.

Clare, I. & Gudjonsson, G. (1995). The vulnerability of suspects with mental retardation during police interviews: A review and experimental study of decision-making. *Mental Handicap Research, 8*(2), 110–128.

Cohen, J. (1969). *Statistical power. Analysis for the behavioural sciences.* New York: Academic Press.

Crane, L., Pring, L., Jukes, K., & Goddard, L. (2012). Patterns of autobiographical memory in adults with autism spectrum disorder. *Journal of Autism and Developmental Disorders, 42*(10), 2100–2112.

Cronbach, L. (1950). Further evidence on response sets and test design. *Educational and Psychological Measurement, 10*, 3–31.

Davis, T., Fodstad, J., Jenkins, W., Hess, J., Moree, B., & Dempsey, T. (2010). Anxiety and avoidance in infants and toddlers with autism spectrum disorders: Evidence for differing symptom severity and presentation. *Research in Autism Spectrum Disorders, 4*, 305–313.

Drake, K. (2014). The role of trait anxiety in the association between the reporting of negative life events and interrogative suggestibility. *Personality and Individual Differences, 60*, 54–59.

Durcan, G. (2021). *The future of prison mental health care in England: A national consultation and review.* www.centreformentalhealth.org.uk/publications/future-prison-mental-health care-england

Ellis, H. & Ashbrook, P. (1988). Resource allocation model of the effects of depressed mood states on memory. In K. Fiedler & J. Forgas (Eds.), *Affect, cognition and social behaviour* (pp. 25–43). Gottingen: Hogrefe.

Engle, R. & Kane, M. (2004). Executive attention, working memory capacity, and a two-factor theory of cognitive control. *Psychology of Learning and Motivation, 44*, 145–200.

Eysenck, M. & Calvo, M. (1992). Anxiety and performance: The processing efficiency theory. *Cognitive and Emotion, 6*, 409–434.

Eysenck, M., Derakshan, N., Santos, R., & Calvo, M. (2007). Anxiety and cognitive performance: Attentional control theory. *Emotion, 7*, 336–353.

Farrugia, L. & Gabbert, F. (2019). Vulnerable suspects in police interviews: Exploring current practice in England and Wales. *Journal of Investigative Psychology and Offender Profiling, 17*(1), 17–30.

Finlay, W. & Lyons, E. (2002). Acquiescence in interviews with people who have mental retardation. *Mental Retardation, 40*(1), 14–29.

Fusar-Poli, P., Deste, G., Smieskova, R., Barlati, S., Yung, A., & Howes, O. (2012). Cognitive functioning in prodromal psychosis: A meta-analysis. *Archives of General Psychiatry, 69*(6), 562–571.

Goodman, G., Christin, O., McWilliams, K., Narr, R., & Paz-Alonso, P. (2014). Memory development in the forensic context. In P. Bauer & R. Fivush (Eds.), *The Wiley handbook on the development of children's memory* (1st ed., pp. 921–961). York: John Wiley.

Gotlib, I. & Joorman, J. (2010). Cognition and depression: Current status and future directions. *Annual Review of Clinical Psychology, 6*, 285–312.

Gudjonsson, G. (1984). A new scale of interrogative suggestibility. *Personality and Individual Differences, 5*, 303–314.

Gudjonsson, G. (1987). A parallel form of the Gudjonsson suggestibility form. *British Journal of Clinical Psychology, 26*, 215–221.

Gudjonsson, G. (1990). The relationship of intellectual skills to suggestibility, compliance and acquiescence. *Personality and Individual Differences, 11*(3), 227–231.

Gudjonsson, G. (1992). *The psychology of interrogations, confessions and testimony.* Chichester: John Wiley.

Gudjonsson, G. (1997). *The Gudjonsson suggestibility scales manual.* Hove: Psychology Press.

Gudjonsson, G. (2010). Psychological vulnerabilities during police interviews. Why are they important? *Legal and Criminological Psychology*, *15*, 161–175.

Gudjonsson, G. (2018). *The psychology of false confessions: Forty years of science and practice.* West Sussex: John Wiley.

Gudjonsson, G. & Clark, N. (1986). Suggestibility in police interrogation: A social psychological model. *Social Behaviour*, *1*, 83–104.

Gudjonsson, G. & Sigurdsson, J. (2004). The relationship of suggestibility and compliance with self-deception and other deception. *Psychology, Crime and Law*, *10*(4), 447–453.

Gudjonsson, G. & Sigurdsson, J. (2010). The relationship of compliance with inattention and hyperactivity/impulsivity. *Personality and Individual Differences*, *49*(6), 651–654.

Gudjonsson, G., Sigurdsson, J., Asgeirsdottir, B., & Sigfusdottir, I. (2007). Custodial interrogation: What are the background factors associated with claimed false confessions? *Journal of Forensic Psychiatry and Psychology*, *18*, 266–275.

Guimond, S., Hawco, C., & Lepage, M. (2017). Prefrontal activity and impaired memory encoding strategies in schizophrenia. *Journal of Psychiatric Research*, *91*, 64–73.

Guo, J., Ragland, R., & Carter, C. (2019). Memory and cognition in schizophrenia. *Molecular Psychiatry*, *24*(5), 633–642.

Hallgren, K. (2012). Computing inter-rater reliability for observational data: An overview and tutorial. *Tutorials in Quantitative Methods for Psychology*, *8*(1), 23–34.

Heal, L. & Sigelman, C. (1995). Response biases in interviews of individuals with limited mental ability. *Journal of Mental Retardation Research*, *39*(3), 331–340.

Herrington, V. & Roberts, K. (2012). Addressing psychological vulnerability in the police suspect interview. *Policing*, *6*, 1–10.

Hertel, P. (1998). Relation between rumination and impaired memory in dysphoric moods. *Journal of Abnormal Psychology*, *107*, 166–172.

Hertel, P. (2004). Memory for emotional and nonemotional events in depression: A question of habit? In D. Reisberg & P. Hertel (Eds.), *Memory and emotion* (pp. 186–216). New York: Oxford University Press.

Hertel, P. & Rude, S. (1991). Depressive deficits in memory: Focusing attention improves subsequent recall. *Journal of Experimental Psychology: General*, *120*, 301–309.

Javeline, D. (1999). Response effects in police cultures: A test of acquiescence in Kazakhstan. *Public Opinion Quarterly*, *63*, 1–28.

Jonides, J., Lewis, R., Nee, D., Lustig, C., Berman, M., & Moore, K. (2008). The mind and brain of short-term memory. *Annual Review of Psychology*, *59*, 193–224.

Kingdon, D. & Turkington, D. (2005). *Cognitive therapy for schizophrenia.* New York: Guildford.

Kleider-Offutt, H., Clevinger, A., & Bond, A. (2016). Working memory and cognitive load in the legal system: Influences on police shooting decisions, interrogation and jury decisions. *Journal of Applied Research in Memory and Cognition, 5*(4), 426–433.

Knowles, E. & Condon, C. (1999). Why do people say "Yes": A dual-process theory of acquiescence. *Journal of Personality and Social Psychology, 77*(2), 379–386.

Koo, T. & Li, M. (2016). A guideline of selecting and reporting intraclass correlation coefficients for reliability research. *Journal of Chiropractic Medicine, 15*(2), 155–163.

Lemogne, C., Piolino, P., Friszer, S., Claret, A., Girault, N., Jouvent, R., Allilaire, J., & Fossati, P. (2006). Episodic autobiographical memory in depression: Specificity, autonetic consciousness, and self perspective. *Consciousness and Cognition, 15*, 258–268.

Lindstrom, B. & Bohlin, G. (2012). Threat-relevance impairs executive functions: Negative impact on working memory and response inhibition. *Emotion, 12*, 384–393.

Macleod, C. & Mathews, A. (2012). Cognitive bias modification approaches to anxiety. *Annual Review of Clinical Psychology, 8*, 189–217.

Maras, K. & Bowler, D. (2010). The cognitive interview for eyewitnesses with autism spectrum disorder. *Journal of Autism and Developmental Disorders, 40*(11), 1350–1360.

Maras, K. & Bowler, D. (2011). Brief report: Schema consistent misinformation effects in eyewitnesses with autism spectrum disorder. *Journal of Autism and Developmental Disorders, 41*, 815–820.

Maras, K., Gaigg, S., & Bowler, D. (2012). Memory for emotionally arousing events over time in autism spectrum disorder. *Emotion, 12*, 1118–1128.

Maras, K., Memon, A., Lambrechts, A., & Bowler, D. (2013). Recall of a live and personally experienced eyewitness event by adults with autism spectrum disorder. *Journal of Autism and Developmental Disorders, 43*, 1798–1810.

Mathews, A. & MacLeod, C. (2005). Cognitive vulnerability to emotional disorders. *Annual Review of Clinical Psychology, 1*, 167–195.

Matikka, L. & Vesala, H. (1997). Acquiescence in quality-of-life interviews with adults who have mental retardation. *Mental Retardation, 35*(2), 75–82.

Narchet, F., Meissner, C., & Russano, M. (2011). Modelling the influence of investigator bias on the elicitation of true and false confessions. *Law and Human Behaviour, 35*, 452–465.

Office for National Statistics. (2021). *Coronavirus and depression in adults, Great Britain: July to August 2021.* London: Office for National Statistics.

Oxburgh, L., Gabbert, F., Milne, R., & Cherryman, J. (2016). Police officers' perceptions and experiences with MD suspects. *International Journal of Law and Psychiatry, 49*, 138–146.

Oxburgh, G., Myklebust, T., & Grant, T. (2010). The question of question types in police interviews: A review of the literature from a psychological and linguistic perspective. *International Journal of Speech, Language and the Law, 17*, 45–66.

Oxburgh, G. & Ost, J. (2011). The use and efficacy of empathy in police interviews with suspects of sexual offences. *Journal of Investigative Psychology and Offender Profiling, 8,* 178–188.

Oxburgh, G., Ost, J., & Cherryman, J. (2012). Police interviews with suspected child sex offenders: Does use of empathy and question type influence the amount of investigation relevant information obtained? *Psychology, Crime and Law, 18,* 259–273.

Perlman, N., Ericson, K., Esses, V., & Isaacs, B. (1994). The developmentally handicapped witness: Competency as a function of question format. *Law and Human Behaviour, 18,* 171–187.

Powell, M. (2002). Specialist training in investigative and evidential interviewing: Is it having any effect on the behaviour of professionals in the field? *Psychiatry, Psychology and Law, 9,* 44–55.

Ragland, J., Laird, A., Ranganath, C., Blumenfeld, R., Gonzales, S., & Glahn, D. (2009). Prefrontal activation deficits during episodic memory in schizophrenia. *American Journal of Psychiatry, 166*(8), 863–874.

Ray, J. (1983). Reviving the problem of acquiescent response bias. *Journal of Social Psychology, 121,* 81–96.

Robinson, O., Vytal, K., Cornwell, B., & Grillon, C. (2013). The impact of anxiety upon cognition: Perspectives from human threat of shock studies. *Frontiers in Human Neuroscience, 7,* 1–20.

Royal College of Psychiatrists. (2017). *Schizophrenia: Information for parents, carers and anyone who works with young people.* www.rcpsych.ac.uk/healthadvice/parentsandyouthinfo/parentscarers/schizophrenia.aspx

Rude, S., Wenzlaff, R., Gibbs, B., Vane, J., & Whitney, T. (2002). Negative processing biases predict subsequent depressive symptoms. *Cognition and Emotion, 16,* 423–440.

Shaw, J. & Budd, E. (1982). Determinants of acquiescence and naysaying of mentally retarded persons. *American Journal of Mental Deficiency, 87*(1), 108–110.

Sigelman, C. & Budd, E. (1986). Pictures as an aid in questioning mentally retarded persons. *Rehabilitation Counselling Bulletin, 29,* 173–181.

Sigelman, C., Winer, J., & Schoenrick, C. (1982). The responsiveness of mentally retarded persons to questions. *Education and Training of the Mentally Retarded, 17,* 120–124.

Sirdifield, C. & Brooker, C. (2012). Detainees in police custody: results of a health needs assessment in Northumbria, England. *International Journal of Prisoner Health, 8,* 60–67.

Snook, B. & Keating, K. (2010). A field study of adult witness interviewing practices in a Canadian police organisation. *Legal and Criminological Psychology, 16,* 160–172.

Strayer, D. & Drews, F. (2007). Cell-phone-induced driver distraction. *Current Directions in Psychological Science, 16*(3), 128–131.

Ternes, M. & Yuille, J. (2008). Eyewitness memory and eyewitness identification performance in adults with intellectual disabilities. *Journal of Applied Research in Intellectual Disabilities, 21,* 519–531.

Tyler, N., Miles, H., Karadag, B., & Rogers, G. (2019). An updated picture of the mental health needs of male and female prisoners in the UK: prevalence, comorbidity, and gender differences. *Social Psychiatry and Psychiatric Epidemiology, 54*, 1143–1152.

Vagni, M., Maiorano, T., & Giostra, V. (2021). The relationship between suggestibility, fabrication, distortion, and trauma in suspected sexually abused children. *Social Sciences, 10*, 37–52.

van Merrienboer, J. & Sweller, J. (2010). Cognitive load theory in health professional education: design principles and strategies. *Medical Education, 44*(1), 85–93.

Vytal, K., Cornwell, B., Arkin, N., & Grillon, C. (2012). Describing the interplay between anxiety and cognition: From impaired performance under low cognitive load to reduced anxiety under high load. *Psychophysiology, 49*, 842–852.

Vytal, K., Cornwell, B., Arkin, N., Letkiewicz, A., Grillon, C. (2013). The complex interaction between anxiety and cognition: Insight from spatial and verbal working memory. *Frontiers in Human Neuroscience, 7*, 93.

Wald, I., Degnan, K., Gorodetsky, E., Charney, D., Fox, N., & Fruchter, E. (2013). Attention to threats and combat-related posttraumatic stress symptoms. *JAMA Psychiatry, 70*, 401–408.

White, T., Schmidt, M., & Karatekin, C. (2010). Verbal and visuospatial working memory development and deficits in children and adolescents with schizophrenia. *Early Intervention in Psychiatry, 4*(4), 305–313.

Williams, J. (1996). Depression and the specificity of autobiographical memory. In D. Rubin (Ed.), *Remembering our past: Studies in autobiographical memory* (pp. 244–267). London: Cambridge University Press.

Williams, J., Barnhofer, T., Crane, C., Herman, D., & Raes, F. (2007). Autobiographical memory specificity and emotional disorder. *Psychological Bulletin, 133*, 122–148.

Williamson, T. (2006). *Investigative interviewing: Rights, research, regulation.* Devon: Willan.

6 A Paradigm Shift

One Size Does *Not* Fit All?

Conducting investigative interviews with suspects with mental health conditions and disorders is difficult (Herrington & Roberts, 2012). Not only do such vulnerable individuals present with their own specific cognitive difficulties, but they may also display increased levels of suggestibility, compliance, and acquiescence – psychological constructs that may lead to them providing misleading or inaccurate information or falsely implicating themselves (Gudjonsson, 2018). As such, it is essential that the investigative interview matches their cognitive abilities (Powell, 2002).

Typically, any suspect interview in England and Wales will start by cautioning the suspect and informing them of their rights. The suspect will be informed of the reason for the interview as well as the objectives and expectations (College of Policing, 2020). Next, the interviewers will seek a free recall, followed by a series of more probing questions concerning the details and topics provided during the free recall. In doing so, the use of appropriate questions should be utilised so that as much accurate and reliable information can be obtained without influencing the suspects' memory – this is particularly important for those at a heightened risk of falsely implicating themselves, such as suspects with mental health conditions and disorders. However, currently, the PEACE model of interviewing is the only theoretically driven interview framework in England and Wales (Williamson, 2006) despite an emerging branch of research that suggests that current interviewing methods, primarily the technique concerning the free recall and the use of open questions (the 'A' of the PEACE model; PEACE is a mnemonic for the five stages of the interview model: Planning and preparation; Engage and explain; Account, clarify, and challenge; Closure; and Evaluation), not being suitable for vulnerable interviewees. Given the lack of research that explores this within a vulnerable suspect group, emerging findings from a vulnerable witness perspective will be drawn upon in respect to

DOI: 10.4324/9781003161028-6

different interview techniques and questioning methods that constitute the 'Account, clarify and challenge' stage of the PEACE model.

The Cognitive Interview and Vulnerability

The Cognitive Interview (CI; Fisher & Geiselman, 1992) was originally developed to provide interviewers with a systematic approach to interviewing in order to elicit the maximum amount of information from witnesses. Based on general principles of cognition, it is now the most commonly used interview method underpinned by vast amounts of empirical research (Dando et al., 2011; Holliday et al., 2011; Richards & Milne, 2018). In its original form, the CI consisted of four basic principles:

(i) *mental reinstatement of context:* encourages the witness to place themselves back at the scene of the crime and mentally recreate the psychological and physical environment. The witness is assisted by the interviewer who asks them to focus on the environmental aspects of the scene, their emotions at the time, and to draw on their senses, for example, asking witnesses to remember what they can see, hear, or smell. Such a technique draws on the encoding specificity principle (Tulving & Thomson, 1973) that highlights that a cue will be effective in memory retrieval if the cue was specifically encoded at the time. As such, asking a witness to place themselves back at the scene of the crime increases the overlap between the recall context and the context of acquisition (Memon & Higham, 1999).

(ii) *report everything:* this principle encourages the witness to report as much detail about what they witnessed even if they believe the detail to be irrelevant including any partial details.

(iii) *change order:* during this stage, the witness is encouraged to recall the witnessed crime from different starting points such as the end, or from the middle. This principle is utilised as it is assumed that a change in retrieval may lead to the recalling of additional details.

(iv) *change perspective:* encouraging a witness to recall from a variety of perspectives such as another witness or the victim, forces a change in retrieval description thus leading to new information being recalled from that other perspective. This allows for multiple pathways to retrieval to be utilised and to an increase in the amount of detail recalled. (See Fisher & Geiselman, 1992, for a full discussion.)

Early research has examined the efficacy of the CI by testing the effectiveness of each of its components. For example, Milne (1997) found that the mental reinstatement of context (MRC) was the most effective component of the CI. Such findings have been consistently established in more recent research concerning children and adults (Dando et al., 2011; Dornburg & McDaniel, 2006; Holliday et al., 2011) and the CI is now a well-established interview technique (Richards & Milne, 2018).

The use of the CI with vulnerable populations, however, has produced different findings. For example, in work involving witnesses with an Autism Spectrum Condition (ASC), the CI was found to be less effective (Maras & Bowler, 2010). In their study, 26 adults with an ASC and 26 typically developing adults viewed a video of a crime after which they were interviewed using either a CI or a structured interview but without the CI techniques. Despite there being no significant differences in the quantity and quality of information between the two witness groups when they were interviewed using a structured interview, the adults with an ASC were significantly less accurate in their recall when they were interviewed using the CI. As such, the Sketch-Reinstatement of Context (Sketch-RC) was developed as an alternative to elements of the CI, such as the MRC. Based on the Task Support Hypothesis (Bowler et al., 1997) which suggests that performance could be improved when there is an uncomplicated retrieval support, this technique involves a few simple instructions with the witness dictating the pace of recall. The Sketch-RC has been found to be effective with those with an ASC (Mattison et al., 2015) as well as with typically developing individuals (Dando et al., 2011; Gental et al., 2014). However, it should be noted that other research suggests that whilst accuracy is improved from individuals with an ASC, the number of correct details was not (Mattison et al., 2018). Thus, its efficiency with all populations is still yet to be fully investigated.

The Self-Administered Interview and Vulnerability

The Self-Administered Interview (SAI; Gabbert et al., 2009), a modified version of the CI, is a tool designed to protect the quality of witness memory. Quite often, the time between witnessing the event and providing an account to the police can be significant given increasing demands placed on police resources (Gabbert et al., 2012). This can lead to issues with recall and pose risks regarding memory contamination due to post-event information (e.g., see Loftus et al., 1992). As such, having a tool that is able to capture an account as soon as possible after the witnessed event serves to reduce the risk of these memory issues and the impact for the ongoing investigation.

The SAI is a recently developed tool that has been designed to capture as much information from witnesses immediately or as soon as possible after the witnessed event. A standardised protocol of instructions, the SAI is a booklet that contains information and instructions to enable witnesses to provide their own free recall in the absence of an interviewing officer (Dando et al., 2020). Adopting the use of memory retrieval techniques, the SAI is suitable for obtaining information from all types of witnesses regarding a range of witnessed crimes (Gabbert et al., 2012). Early research work found that the SAI assists with the retrieval of accurate information as well as protecting eyewitness memory and minimising forgetting (Gabbert et al., 2009). This is in line with existing knowledge regarding memory and retrieval in that an early retrieval enhances retention and later recall of information due to the creation of different retrieval routes that accesses the originally encoded information (Dempster, 1997; Schacter et al., 1998). This can lead to a reduction in the impact of post-event misinformation on memory recall (Loftus et al., 1992). More recent research has continuously provided support for the SAI protecting the quantity and quality of information from witnesses (Gabbert et al., 2012), including adults of all ages (Dando et al., 2020; Gawrylowicz et al., 2014; Hope et al., 2011; Matsuo & Miura, 2016).

Research regarding the use of the SAI with vulnerable populations is limited however (Hargie, 2018). Recent work conducted by Maras et al. (2014) examined whether the use of the SAI is more useful than the CI in witnesses that have an ASC. Their results overall found that the SAI did not elicit more correct details when compared to a written interview with witnesses that have an ASC. Furthermore, specific elements, such as the MRC, in the SAI did not improve recall compared with a structured recall interview, thus suggesting in line with previous research that the CI mnemonics (albeit adapted in the SAI) are ineffective with this type of vulnerable group (Maras & Bowler, 2012). However, Maras et al. (2014) also reported that the sketch element of the SAI did elicit more correct details when compared to the section that asked for written descriptions of the witnessed scene, although it must be noted that this benefit was experienced to a lesser degree in the witnesses with an ASC compared to the control group. Such findings raise important implications for the investigative interviewing of this vulnerable group, particularly in relation to the sketch element, and the consideration of drawing as a tool to assist with alleviating the demands of cognitive load concerned with memory and recall. To date, there has been little (if any) other research that has explored the use of the SAI with other vulnerable populations.

The Witness-Aimed First Account

Research is emerging that suggests that the current police interviewing techniques do not take into account specific difficulties associated with individuals that have an ASC, and that such witnesses recall significantly less information when a free narrative approach is used (Almeida et al., 2019; Maras & Bowler, 2010, 2011, 2012; Mattison et al., 2018). As such, the Witness-Aimed First Account (WAFA; Maras et al., 2020) has recently been developed as an interview technique for witnesses that have an ASC with an emphasis on supporting the differences in the way in which such witnesses attend to and process information into memory. Given that research has suggested that those with an ASC perform better at retrieval when they are provided with specific guidance (Bowler et al., 2014; Losh & Capps, 2003), the WAFA provides directive prompts. In this interview technique, witnesses provide their own free recall by breaking it down into segments. Here the interviewer initially asks the witness, "In just a couple of sentences or a few words, what was the most important event that happened?" Following the witness response, they are prompted again, "Tell me something else that happened." Each time the witness provides a segment or topic, the interviewer records this on a post-it note. This provides the witness with a prompt of the structure of the witnessed event. After the witness has provided all of the topics, the interviewer revisits each of the topics on the post-it notes in turn. This allows the witness to focus on each segment at a time and, using their own search and retrieval strategies, recall as much information as they can from each parameter-bound topic, before they are probed for any final detail. The WAFA interview concludes with a closure stage.

Research testing the WAFA is in its infancy given the recent development of the interview technique. To date, only one study has explored its efficiency as an interview technique for witnesses with an ASC. Maras and colleagues (2020) recruited a sample of 63 individuals, of which 30 were categorised as typically developing and 33 were diagnosed with an ASC. Participants were instructed to watch two videos depicting either a handbag theft or a fight in a bar and were interviewed using either the WAFA technique or a control interview that consisted of a free recall and follow up open questions. Qualitative feedback was also sought from the participants following their engagement with the interview. Their study revealed some interesting findings. Although those with an

ASC tended to recall fewer correct details overall when compared to the typically developing participants when using the WAFA technique, the completeness of participants' episodic recall improved significantly in both groups of participants. The qualitative feedback reported that the WAFA interview technique had led participants to think harder and remember more, with participants feeling more comfortable overall. As such, Maras and colleagues have produced positive findings that suggest an interview technique specifically for those with an ASC may benefit not only the individual themselves but the overall investigation in terms of obtaining a more complete and a more accurate account. Such bespoke interviewing techniques warrant further attention not only for vulnerable witnesses but also for vulnerable suspects.

An Alternative Approach for Suspects?

Despite the various modifications and new interview techniques that have been developed and explored for vulnerable witnesses, there remains a dearth of work that has explored alternative interview techniques for vulnerable suspects, particularly those with mental health conditions and disorders. Although there has been very little work that specifically investigates suspects with mental health conditions and disorders, scholars have explored vulnerability within the investigative interview through a variety of methods. One method has been through the examination of real-life suspect interview transcripts. This allows for a range of variables to be examined that one may consider important; for example, the frequency of question types (Snook & Keating, 2011), the repeated use of question types (Cederborg et al., 2009; Guadagno & Powell, 2014; Howie et al., 2004; Krahenbuhl, 2007), and the impact of question types on the quality and type of information elicited from the interviewee (Farrugia & Gabbert, 2019; Snook et al., 2012). Such a method allows for an insight into actual investigative interviewing practice which is informative and has high external validity. However, obtaining the data can be problematic, and the data can often be incomplete or difficult to analyse. For example, there is little experimental control and researchers may find it arduous to control for the various different types of crime, the number of interviewers, and the unknown ground truth – that is, the inability to know if the suspect is telling the truth in their account and/or what the true circumstances of the offence may be. As such, this impacts upon the type of analysis that can be conducted – analysing the quality of the information elicited can be difficult if the ground truth is unknown for example (Farrugia & Gabbert, 2019).

Experimental and lab-based studies allow for the manipulation of such variables and others including participant characteristics such as mental health or learning disability (Perlman et al., 1994; Ternes & Yuille, 2008), and the impact of different interview methods upon the reliability of the information obtained (Clarke et al., 2013; Jack et al., 2014). However, as has already been documented in this chapter, such experimental work has rarely been conducted with vulnerable suspects – the latter two studies being work conducted with witnesses. However, these methods allow for experimental control and was the approach that Farrugia and Gabbert (2020) engaged with when considering an alternative interview model for *suspects* with mental health conditions and disorders.

Forensic Interviewing of Mentally Disordered Suspects: The Impact of Interview Style on Investigation Outcomes (Farrugia & Gabbert, 2020)

Aims

Building upon previous research work (see Farrugia & Gabbert, 2019), the aim was to experimentally test two different interview models; a best practice interview containing largely open questions and a modified interview model containing largely closed questions. As such, the following research questions were addressed:

(i)   Which interview model (best practice v modified interview) elicited the most amount of investigation relevant information (IRI) and the most accurate?

(ii) Which interview model (best practice v modified interview) was most appropriate for suspects with mental health conditions and disorders?

Based on the emerging research that suggests alternative interview techniques are required for vulnerable individuals, the following hypotheses were generated:

H1. Participants with mental health conditions and disorders will provide more IRI during the modified interview than the best practice interview.

H2. Participants with mental health conditions and disorders will seek more clarification during best practice interviews than the modified interview.

Given the exploratory nature regarding the accuracy of IRI within a suspect context, no hypotheses were generated for this element. In addition, given that elements of vulnerability have not been well explored within the context of different interview models, no hypotheses were generated for this aspect either.

Method

Ethical approval was gained from the Human Research Ethics Committee of the University of Sunderland.

Sample

A sample of 110 participants were recruited from three universities in England via a purposive sampling method. Participants were only able to participate if they were aged 18 years and over and had a good understanding of English. Those with a Learning Difficulty or Learning Disabilities were excluded; this led to two participants who self-reported a Learning Disability being excluded. The final sample, therefore, consisted of 108 participants (18 male and 90 female), with an average age of 24.1 years ($SD = 7.93$). The sample included those with mental health conditions and disorders, including those that reported co-morbidity ($n = 47$) and those that did not report any existing mental health condition or disorder ($n = 61$). The range of mental health conditions and disorders are in Table 6.1. The participants were split between the two interview conditions and received three research credits via the University's SONA Systems for participating.

Materials

A coding framework and guide was developed based on current interview practice in England and Wales and relevant recent psychological research (Farrugia & Gabbert, 2019). The coding framework consisted of four sections which focused predominately on the 'Account, clarify and challenge' phase of the PEACE model:

Table 6.1 Table of participants' self-reported mental health conditions and disorders

Mental Health Condition or Disorder	N
Depression	13
Anxiety	8
Bipolar Disorder	3
Bulimia	2
Anorexia	1
Borderline Personality Disorder	1
Post-Traumatic Stress Disorder	1
Anxiety and Depression	11
Anxiety and Post-Traumatic Stress Disorder	1
Depression and Obsessive-Compulsive Disorder	1
Anxiety, Depression, and Body Dysmorphic Disorder	1
Anxiety, Depression, and Obsessive-Compulsive Disorder	1
Anxiety, Depression, and Post-Traumatic Stress Disorder	1
Anxiety, Depression, Paranoid Personality Disorder, and Psychosis	1
Anxiety, Obsessive-Compulsive Disorder, and Anorexia	1
Total	47

Source: Farrugia and Gabbert (2020).

(i)   The first section documented general participant demographics and interview characteristics.

(ii) Question typology was recorded in the second section based on current classifications within the literature (see Oxburgh et al., 2010 for a full discussion) and recent research (Farrugia & Gabbert, 2019). This included the number of clarifications sought for each question type.

(iii) The amount of IRI obtained from the participant was recorded in section three in line with previous research (see Farrugia & Gabbert, 2019; Oxburgh et al., 2012). The accuracy of the IRI was also counted in addition to the amount in this section; this was recorded on the basis of correct versus incorrect items of information.

(iv) The final section counted instances of vulnerability portrayed by the participant and related specifically to suggestibility, compliance, and acquiescence as defined in the existing literature (Gudjonsson, 2018).

The coding guide was developed to ensure consistency across all data coding by providing operational definitions for each section of the coding framework.

Procedure

Each participant was provided with an information sheet and consent form before being instructed to complete two tasks: (i) retrieve a mobile phone from a bag and (ii) obtain exam scripts from a laptop. Each task was completed in a designated room on the university campus. Each participant was informed which of their two tasks were classed as the minor transgression and the matched non-transgression so that they understood which task the interviewing officer was 'investigating.' Following the completion of both tasks, each participant engaged in a suspect interview conducted by a serving police officer who had been briefed in both interview models. Participants were randomly allocated to either the best practice interview or the modified interview. The order of tasks and interview method were counterbalanced. Following the completion of the interview, the participant was debriefed and awarded their research credits.

Design

A 2 (participant type: mental health conditions and disorders v no vulnerability) × 2 (interview type: best practice interview v modified interview) between-subjects design was utilised, with the following dependent variables: (i) quantity of IRI, measured by the number of items of information, (ii) accuracy of IRI, measured by the number of correct crime-related items of information, (iii) amount of clarifications, and (iv) level of vulnerability, measured by the sum of instances of suggestibility, compliance, and acquiescence.

Data Analysis

A quarter of the interviews ($n = 27$) were double coded to ensure for inter-rater reliability. Data relating to question type, amount and accuracy of IRI, level of clarifications and the overall vulnerability were coded for the number of instances that they occurred and so were subjected to intraclass correlation; a method recommended for assessing continuous variables (Hallgren, 2012). Correlations were 0.96 and 0.99 for open and closed questions respectively, 0.94 for the overall amount of IRI, and 0.97 for IRI accuracy, 0.97 for clarification of questions, and 0.79 for overall vulnerability, thus demonstrating good to excellent inter-rater reliability (Koo & Li, 2016).

Results

Best Practice Interview v Modified Interview: Amount and Accuracy of IRI

The amount and accuracy of IRI obtained from both participant groups within the two different interview models was explored. A between-subjects ANCOVA was conducted with the overall amount of IRI as the dependent variable, whilst controlling for interview length. There was no significant main effect for participant type, $F(1, 103) = .34$, $p = .56$, $\eta_p^2 = .003$, and no significant main effect for interview type, $F(1, 103) = 1.29$, $p = .26$, $\eta_p^2 = .01$. However, there was a significant interaction between participant type and interview type, $F(1, 103) = 4.40$, $p = .04$, $\eta_p^2 = .04$. Participants with mental health conditions and disorders tended to provide more IRI during the modified interview ($M = 145.86$, $SD = 7.80$) than the best practice interview ($M = 139.02$, $SD = 7.80$). Participants without mental health conditions and disorders tended to provide more IRI during the best practice interview ($M = 150.22$, $SD = 7.02$) than the modified interview ($M = 126.08$, $SD = 6.90$). Simple effects analysis revealed no significant differences in the overall amount of IRI between the two participant groups in the best practice interview, $t(52) = .79$, $p = .22$, or in the modified interview, $t(52) = 1.70$, $p = .99$.

The accuracy of the IRI elicited from the participant groups was also examined. A between-subjects ANCOVA was conducted with the overall amount of correct information as the dependent variable whilst controlling for interview length. There was no significant main effect for participant type, $F(1, 103) = .40$, $p = .53$, $\eta_p^2 = .004$. There was also no significant main effect for interview type, $F(1, 103) = .31$, $p = .58$, $\eta_p^2 = .003$. There was a significant interaction between participant type and interview type, $F(1, 103) = 4.89$, $p = .03$, $\eta_p^2 = .05$. Participants with mental health conditions and disorders tended to provide more correct IRI during the modified interview ($M = 91.41$, $SD = 1.27$) than the best practice interview ($M = 89.49$, $SD = 1.24$). This is in direct contrast to the non-vulnerable participant group; they tended to provide more correct IRI during the best practice interview

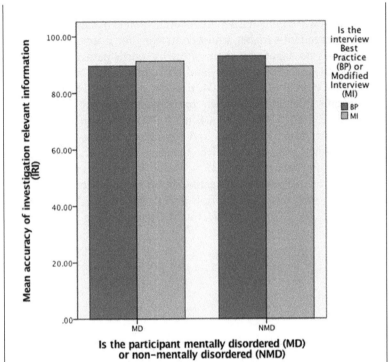

Figure 6.1 Accuracy of IRI in best practice and modified interview models (Farrugia & Gabbert, 2020)

(M = 92.83, SD = 1.11) than the modified interview (M = 89.56, SD = 1.10). Simple effects analysis revealed a significant difference in the accuracy of the IRI obtained between the two participant groups in the best practice interview, t (52) = 2.76, p = .01. Participants without mental health conditions and disorders provided a higher amount of accurate IRI than those with mental health conditions and disorders. However, there was no significant difference in the accuracy levels between the two groups in the modified interview, t (52) = .93, p = .58 (see Figure 6.1).

Best Practice Interview v Modified Interview: Level of Clarifications

The level of clarification sought by both participant groups dependent on interview model was examined. A between-subjects

ANCOVA was conducted with the overall number of classifications as the dependent variable, whilst controlling for interview length. There was no significant main effect for participant type, F (1, 103) = .01, p = .98, η_p^2 = .01, and no significant main effect for interview type, F (1, 103) = .04, p = .84, η_p^2 = .01. There was a significant interaction between participant type and interview type, F (1, 103) = 4.44, p = .04, η_p^2 = .04. That is, participants with mental health conditions and disorders tended to seek more clarification during best practice interviews (M = 1.42, SD = .25) than the modified interview (M = .87, SD = .26). This differed to participants without mental health conditions and disorders; they tended to seek more clarification during the modified interview (M = .92, SD .23). Simple effect analysis revealed no significant

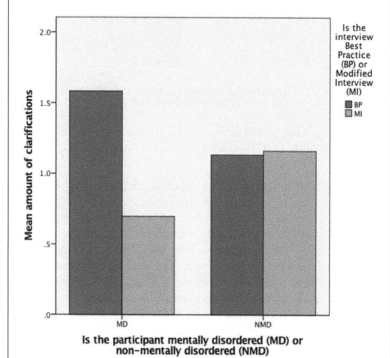

Figure 6.2 Clarifications of questions in best practice and modified interview models (Farrugia & Gabbert, 2020)

differences in the number of clarifications between the two groups in the best practice interview, t (52) = 1.03, p = .92, or in the modified interview, t (52) = 1.29, p = .10 (see Figure 6.2).

Best Practice Interview v Modified Interview: Vulnerability

The final set of analysis explored the level of vulnerability based on suggestibility, compliance, and acquiescence displayed by the two participant groups in each of the interview types. A between-subjects ANCOVA was conducted with the overall level of vulnerability as the dependent variable, whilst controlling for interview length. There was no significant main effect for participant type, F (1, 103) = .90, p = .35, η_p^2 = .01, and no significant main effect for interview type, F (1, 103) = .45, p = .51, η_p^2 = .01. Furthermore, there was no significant interaction between participant type and interview type, F (1, 103) = .51, p = .48, η_p^2 = .01.

Summary

Conducting investigative interviews with vulnerable suspects is challenging. Whilst the literature base regarding interview techniques remains relatively under-developed for suspects with mental health conditions and disorders, there is a rapidly developing level of research being conducted for vulnerable witnesses. For example, the CI has been regularly assessed as a whole for different witness types, as well as its various components. This has led to the realisation that different interview techniques may be needed for different vulnerable witnesses. As such, the CI has been modified and elements replaced such as the MRC with Sketch-Reinstatement of Context. Furthermore, the SAI has been developed to assist with obtaining an account as soon as is practically possible after the witnessed event – this is particularly important given the increasing time between the witnessing of the event and providing a formal account to the police (Gabbert et al., 2012; Kebbell et al., 1999). The SAI also serves to reduce the risk of memory contamination due to post-event information, and the witness forgetting what they have observed. More recently, the WAFA interview technique (Maras et al., 2020) has been developed to assist those specifically with an ASC when they are required to provide a witness account to the police. Initial research has suggested that the completeness of recall (including accuracy) is significantly improved in witness with an ASC and in those without.

What remains missing is the consideration of alternative interview techniques for vulnerable suspects, particularly those that have mental health conditions and disorders. Recent work conducted by Farrugia and Gabbert (2019) examined existing practice and found that current best practice interview methods may not be entirely suitable for suspects with mental health conditions and disorders. The work of Farrugia and Gabbert (2020) sought to build upon this by testing an alternative interview model experimentally. Participants with mental health conditions and disorders tended to provide a higher amount of IRI and more accurate IRI in the modified interview than the best practice interview. Furthermore, the number of clarifications required by the vulnerable suspect were significantly less in the modified interview compared to the best practice interview. This suggests that the use of specific questions, such as those tested in the modified interview, may provide scaffolding for this type of vulnerable suspect and thus reduce the impact on cognitive effort that a free recall, open question interview can impose (White et al., 2009). Adaptations to interview models must take into account the way that a vulnerable suspect perceives, processes, and retrieves information. The findings from Farrugia and Gabbert (2020) continue to challenge whether best practice really is best practice for suspects with mental health conditions and disorders.

Key Learning Points

- Currently, other than the PEACE model of interviewing, there is no alternative framework in England and Wales.
- There is an emerging branch of research that suggests that using a free recall approach and open questions is not suitable for vulnerable interviewees.
- Given the lack of research exploring vulnerable suspects, much of our understanding is derived from literature concerning vulnerable witnesses.
- The use of the CI is limited with some vulnerable witnesses and elements such as Sketch-Reinstatement of Context have been introduced to assist.
- The Self-Administered Interview has also been developed to ensure that memory is not contaminated and that an account can be provided quickly, often at the scene of the witnessed event. Research exploring its use with vulnerable witnesses is limited, however.

- The Witness-Aimed First Account seeks to address the specific difficulties experienced by those with an ASC by using directive prompts and encouraging witnesses to use their own search and retrieval strategies. Early research has shown support for this interview technique.
- There remains little consideration for alternative interview techniques for vulnerable suspects, particularly those that have mental health conditions and disorders.
- The work of Farrugia and Gabbert (2019, 2020) suggests that more specific questioning techniques produces a higher amount and more accurate level of IRI than open questions, whilst reducing confusion.

References

Almeida, T., Lamb, M., & Weisblatt, E. (2019). Effects of delay on episodic memory retrieval by children with autism spectrum disorder. *Applied Cognitive Psychology*, *33*(5), 814–827.

Bowler, D., Gaigg, S., & Gardiner, J. (2014). Binding of multiple features in memory by high-functioning adults with autism spectrum disorder. *Journal of Autism and Developmental Disorders*, *44*, 2355–2362.

Bowler, D., Matthews, N., & Gardiner, J. M. (1997). Asperger's syndrome and memory: similarity to autism but not amnesia. *Neuropsychologia*, *35*, 65–70.

Cederborg, A., Danielsson, H., La Rooy, D., & Lamb, M. (2009). Repetition of contaminating questions types when children and youths with intellectual disabilities are interviewed. *Journal of Intellectual Disability Research*, *53*, 440–449.

Clarke, J., Prescott, K., & Milne, R. (2013). How effective is the cognitive interview when used with adults with intellectual disabilities specifically with conversation recall? Journal of Applied Research in Intellectual Disabilities, 26, 546–556.

College of Policing. (2020). *Investigation. Investigative Interviewing.* www.app.college.police.uk/app-content/investigations/investigativeinterviewing/#engage-and-explain

Dando, C., Gabbert, F., & Hope, L. (2020). Supporting older eyewitnesses' episodic memory: The self-administered interview and sketch reinstatement of context. *Memory*, *28*(6), 712–723.

Dando, C. J., Wilcock, R., Behnkle, C., & Milne, R. (2011). Modifying the cognitive interview: Countenancing forensic application by enhancing practicability. *Psychology, Crime & Law*, *17*, 491–511.

Dempster, F. (1997). Using tests to promote classroom learning. In R. Dillon (Ed.), *Handbook on testing* (pp. 557–580). Chicago: Greenwood Press.

Dornburg, C. C., & McDaniel, M. A. (2006). The cognitive interview enhances long-term free recall of older adults. *Psychology & Aging, 21,* 196–200.

Farrugia, L. & Gabbert, F. (2019). Vulnerable suspects in police interviews: Exploring current practice in England and Wales. *Journal of Investigative Psychology and Offender Profiling, 17*(1), 17–30.

Farrugia, L. & Gabbert, F. (2020). Forensic interviewing of mentally disordered suspects: the impact of interview style on investigation outcomes. *Current Psychology,* 1–9. DOI: https://doi.org/10.1007/s12144-020-00747-8

Fisher, R. & Geiselman, R. (1992). *Memory-enhancing techniques for investigative interviewing: The cognitive interview.* Springfield, IL: Charles C. Thomas.

Gabbert, F., Hope, L., & Fisher, R. (2009). Protecting eyewitness evidence: Examining the efficacy of a self-administered interview tool. *Law and Human Behaviour, 33,* 298–307.

Gabbert, F., Hope, L., Fisher, R., & Jamieson, K. (2012). Protecting against misleading post event information with a self-administered interview. *Applied Cognitive Psychology, 26,* 568–575.

Gawrylowicz, J., Memon, A., & Scoboria, A. (2014). Equipping witnesses with transferable skills: The self-administered interview. *Psychology, Crime and Law, 20*(4), 315–325.

Gentle, M., Powell, M. B., & Sharman, S. J. (2014). Mental context reinstatement or drawing: Which better enhances children's recall of witnessed events and protects against suggestive questions? *Australian Journal of Psychology, 66*(3), 158–167.

Guadagno, B. & Powell, M. (2014). An examination of the prevalence of temporally leading questions in child witness interviews. *International Journal of Police Science and Management, 16*(1), 16–25.

Gudjonsson, G. (2018). *The psychology of false confessions: Forty years of science and practice.* West Sussex: Wiley.

Hallgren, K. (2012). Computing inter-rater reliability for observational data: An overview and tutorial. *Tutorials in Quantitative Methods for Psychology, 8*(1), 23–34.

Hargie, O. (2018). *The handbook of communication skills.* London: Routledge.

Herrington, V. & Roberts, K. (2012). Addressing psychological vulnerability in the police suspect interview. *Policing, 6,* 1–10.

Holliday, R., Humphries, J., Milne, R., Memon, A., Houlder, L., Lyons, A., & Bull, R. (2011). Reducing misinformation effects in older adults with Cognitive Interview mnemonics. *Psychology and Aging, 27*(4), 1191–1203.

Hope, L., Gabbert, F., & Fisher, R. (2011). From laboratory to the street: Capturing witness memory using the Self-Administered Interview. *Legal and Criminological Psychology, 16,* 211–226.

Howie, P., Sheehan, M., Mojarrad, T., & Wrzesinska, M. (2004). 'Undesirable' and 'desirable' shifts in children's responses to repeated questions: Age differences in the effect of providing a rationale for repetition. *Applied Cognitive Psychology, 18,* 1161–1180.

Jack, F., Leov, J. & Zajac, R. (2014). Age-related differences in the free-recall accounts of child, adolescent, and adult witnesses. *Applied Cognitive Psychology*, *28*, 30–38.

Kebbell, M., Milne, R., & Wagstaff, G. (1999). The cognitive interview: A survey of its forensic effectiveness. *Psychology, Crime and Law*, *5*, 101–115.

Koo, T. & Li, M. (2016). A guideline of selecting and reporting intraclass correlation coefficients for reliability research. *Journal of Chiropractic Medicine*, *15*(2), 155–163.

Krahenbuhl, S. (2007). *The effect of question repetition on young children's eyewitness testimony*. Unpublished doctoral dissertation. University of Sheffield, UK.

Loftus, E., Levidow, B., & Duensing, S. (1992). Who remembers best? Individual differences in memory for events that occurred in a science museum. *Applied Cognitive Psychology*, *6*, 93–107.

Losh, M. & Capps, L. (2003). Narrative ability in high-functioning children with autism or Asperger's syndrome. *Journal of Autism and Developmental Disorders*, *33*(3), 239–251.

Maras, K. & Bowler, D. (2010). The cognitive interview for eyewitnesses with autism spectrum disorder. *Journal of Autism and Developmental Disorders*, *40*(11), 1350–1360.

Maras, K. & Bowler, D. (2011). Brief report: Schema consistent misinformation effects in eyewitnesses with autism spectrum disorder. *Journal of Autism and Developmental Disorders*, *41*, 815–820.

Maras, K. & Bowler, D. (2012). Context reinstatement effects on eyewitness memory in autism spectrum disorder. *British Journal of Psychology*, *103*(3), 330–342.

Maras, K., Dando, C., Stephenson, H., Lambrechts, A., Anns, S., & Gaigg, S. (2020). The witness-aimed first account (WAFA): A new technique for interviewing autistic witnesses and victims. *Autism*, *24*(6), 1449–1467.

Maras, K., Mulcahy, S., Memon, A., Picariello, F., & Bowler, D. (2014). Evaluating the effectiveness of the self-administered interview for witnesses with autism spectrum disorder. *Applied Cognitive Psychology*, *28*, 693–701.

Matsuo, K. & Miura, H. (2016). Effectiveness of the self-administered interview and drawing pictures for eliciting eyewitness memories. *Psychiatry, Psychology and Law*, *24*(5), 643–654.

Mattison, M., Dando, C., & Ormerod, T. (2015). Sketching to remember: Episodic free recall task support fort child witnesses and victims with autism spectrum disorder. *Journal of Autism and Developmental Disorders*, *45*, 1751–1765.

Mattison, M., Dando, C., & Ormerod, T. (2018). Drawing the answers: Sketching to support free and probed recall by child witnesses and victims with autism spectrum disorder. *Autism*, *22*(2), 181–194.Memon, A. & Higham, P. (1999). A review of the cognitive interview. *Psychology, Crime and Law*, *5*(1–2), 177–196.

Milne, R. (1997). *Application and analysis of the cognitive interview*. Doctoral Dissertation. University of Portsmouth.

Oxburgh, G., Myklebust, T., & Grant, T. (2010). The question of question types in police interviews: A review of the literature from a psychological and linguistic perspective. *International Journal of Speech, Language and the Law, 17*, 45–66.

Oxburgh, G., Ost, J., & Cherryman, J. (2012). Police interviews with suspected child sex offenders: Does use of empathy and question type influence the amount of investigation relevant information obtained? *Psychology, Crime and Law, 18*, 259–273.

Perlman, N., Ericson, K., Esses, V., & Isaacs, B. (1994). The developmentally handicapped witness: Competency as a function of question format. *Law and Human Behaviour, 18*, 171–187.

Powell, M. (2002). Specialist training in investigative and evidential interviewing: Is it having any effect on the behaviour of professionals in the field? *Psychiatry, Psychology and Law, 9*, 44–55.

Richards, J. & Milne, R. (2018). The cognitive interview and its use for people with autism spectrum disorder: Can we create an ASD friendly version? In J. Johnson, G. Goodman, and P. Mundy (Eds.), *The Wiley handbook of memory, autism spectrum disorder, and the law* (pp. 245–269). London: Wiley Blackwell.

Schacter, D., Norman, K., & Koutstaal, W. (1998). The cognitive neuroscience of constructive memory. *Annual Review of Psychology, 49*, 289–318.

Snook, B. & Keating, K. (2011). A field study of adult witness interviewing practices in a Canadian police organisation. *Legal and Criminological Psychology, 16*(1), 160–172.

Snook, B., Luther, K., Quinlan, H., & Milne, R. (2012). Let 'em talk! A field study of police questioning practices of suspects and accused persons. *Criminal Justice and Behaviour, 39*(10), 1328–1339.

Ternes, M. & Yuille, J. (2008). Eyewitness memory and eyewitness identification performance in adults with intellectual disabilities. *Journal of Applied Research in Intellectual Disabilities, 21*, 519–531.

Tulving, E., & Thomson, D. M. (1973). Encoding specificity and retrieval processes in episodic memory. *Psychological Review, 80*, 352–373.

White, S., Burgess, P., & Hill, E. (2009). Impairments on "open-ended" executive function tests in autism. *Autism Research, 2*(3), 138–147.

Williamson, T. (2006). *Investigative interviewing: Rights, research, regulation.* Devon: Willan.

7   New Directions
Implications and Future Research

From Interrogation to Investigative Interviewing

The move from the confession-seeking ethos bolstered by many early interrogation manuals and methods is undoubtedly one of the most significant improvements in modern-day policing. One such technique, known as the Reid Interrogation Technique (Inbau et al., 2013) was originally developed in the 1970s. It was this particular approach that has since been viewed as a major cause of false confessions in a number of miscarriages of justice (Gudjonsson, 2018; Kassin, 2005). Whilst it can be difficult to imagine that an innocent individual would falsely confess to a crime, these are well documented in the literature (Drizin & Leo, 2004; Gudjonsson, 2018) and there now exists a taxonomy that distinguishes between three different types of false confessions (see Kassin & Wrightsman, 1985).

It was the case of Maxwell Confait that highlighted the impact of inappropriate interviewing methods on the likelihood of inducing a false confession (Price & Caplan, 1977). Leading to the Fisher Inquiry (Fisher, 1977) and the Royal Commission on Criminal Procedure (RCCP, 1981), new legislation was introduced that provided a legislative framework for the use of police powers. The Police and Criminal Evidence Act (PACE, 1984) and associated Codes of Practice ensured that interviews were audio-recorded, and that legal advice was offered to all suspects. However, interviewing remained poor, and it was not until the introduction of the PEACE model of interviewing (Williamson, 2006), that practices moved away from the previous interrogatory nature to a more investigative interviewing approach.

Based upon psychological research, the PEACE model of interviewing emphasises obtaining accurate and reliable information and is underpinned by seven key principles to encourage good investigative interviewing. However, an extensive body of psychological

DOI: 10.4324/9781003161028-7

research has produced mixed results in terms of officers demonstrating appropriate interviewing methods (Clarke & Milne, 2001; Griffiths & Milne, 2006; G. Oxburgh et al., 2010a, 2010b; Soukara et al., 2009; Walsh & Milne, 2008; Walsh & Bull, 2010; Wright & Powell, 2006), with a particular focus on appropriate questioning techniques. Although there is some discussion within the psychological literature in categorising question types (see G. Oxburgh et al., 2010a for a review), the general consensus is that open and probing questions tend to produce longer, more detailed and more accurate information when compared to questions deemed as inappropriate, such as the use of closed or leading questions (Griffiths & Milne, 2006; Myklebust, 2009; Phillips et al., 2011; Snook et al., 2012). However, the reality is that many officers still commonly use more closed questions than open questions (Farrugia & Gabbert, 2019b; Snook & Keating, 2011; Wright & Alison, 2004).

Alongside the implementation of PACE (1984) and the PEACE model of interviewing, the College of Policing have also introduced the Professionalising Investigation Programme (PIP) to replace the previously used five-tiered structure of interviewing skills, and Authorised Professional Practice (APP; College of Policing, 2018) that provides guidance on all elements of policing, including the investigation and interviewing stages. Furthermore, all serving police officers are encouraged to follow the National Decision Model (NDM; College of Policing, 2014) in conducting their day-to-day activities. Consequently, today's interviewing practices in England and Wales are unrecognisable from the confession-seeking ethos of the past.

The Concept of Vulnerability and the Vulnerable Suspect

Vulnerability within the criminal justice system (CJS) is not a new phenomenon (L. Oxburgh et al., 2016). However, despite this being a key concern across policing and public health partners (Murray et al., 2018), there does not appear to be a unified definition of vulnerability across (Bull, 2010). Within the psychological literature, it is the work of Gudjonsson that has been most influential in defining and addressing vulnerability within a policing context. Defined as "psychological characteristics or mental state which renders an [individual] prone, in certain circumstances, to providing information which is inaccurate, unreliable or misleading" (Gudjonsson, 2006, p.68), Gudjonsson identifies four main types of psychological vulnerability – mental disorder being one of them. Within the context of policing, it is the PACE (1984), in particular, Code C (2018) that provides requirements for the detention, treatment, and questioning of suspects, including those that are vulnerable, and the Youth Justice and Criminal Evidence Act (1999) and Achieving Best Evidence in Criminal Proceedings (Ministry of Justice, 2011) that sets out guidance on how to use Special Measures for victims and witnesses that are intimidated or vulnerable.

Despite the increasing awareness of vulnerability, suspects that have mental health conditions and disorders are often perceived by many as dangerous and unpredictable (Daff & Thomas, 2014), and there are numerous debates regarding these vulnerable individuals being responsible for a disproportionate level of serious and violent crimes (Neumann & Hare, 2008), and presenting a greater risk of criminal recidivism (Douglas et al., 2006). The Criminalisation Hypothesis (Abrahamson, 1972), for example, describes the overrepresentation of those with ill mental health in the CJS, although there is a growing body of literature that challenges this assumption (Case et al., 2009; Fisher et al., 2006; Junginger et al., 2006; Peterson et al., 2010). In addition, a number of psychological theories also describes how our perceptions influence our subsequent interactions with such vulnerable individuals (e.g., Schema Theory [Anderson, 1977], and Labelling Theory [Link et al., 1999; Scheff, 1984]). The work of L. Oxburgh et al. (2016) explored this further by investigating police officers' perceptions of interviewing suspects with mental health conditions and disorders. Their findings, conceptualised by the Police Experience Transitional Model, suggest that these vulnerable suspects are generally still viewed negatively and that there may need to be a change in questioning strategy to assist with their level of understanding. This has serious implications for how these vulnerable suspects may be treated; the way a police officer perceives this type of vulnerable suspect will impact upon their subsequent interaction and treatment of that individual, due to the myths, stereotypes, and beliefs that the mental health/disorder label can evoke (Link et al., 1999; Scheff, 1966). There are also implications for the co-operation of the suspect; Procedural Justice Theory (Tyler & Blader, 2003) suggests that individuals are more likely to cooperate with 'authority figures' if they feel that they have been treated fairly, given an opportunity to voice their opinions and afforded dignity and respect. This suggests that the treatment and outcomes of suspects with mental health conditions or disorders is heavily dependent on whom they encounter and their perceptions (Cant & Standen, 2007).

Given that individuals with mental health conditions and disorders are over-represented in custody in England and Wales (Fazel & Seewald, 2012; McKinnon & Grubin, 2010), the need for appropriate and effective identification of such vulnerabilities is critical. Although the College of Policing (2017) has developed APP to assist officers in identifying vulnerability upon a suspect first entering custody, research has consistently documented the difficulties in doing so (Baksheev et al., 2012; Gudjonsson, 2010; Kassin, 2012; McKinnon & Grubin, 2013; Noga et al., 2015). Whilst this may be due to some individuals masking their difficulties, others have suggested that the screening tools used are not 'fit for purpose' (McKinnon & Grubin, 2013, 2014; Young et al., 2013) and refer to the little to no formal training received by custody officers in mental health (Bather et al., 2008).

This has implications for the implementation of the relevant safeguards afforded to vulnerable suspects; if an individual's vulnerabilities are not appropriately identified, they will not be provided with the necessary safeguards. Whilst vulnerable suspects can be assisted by intermediaries, such a direction is yet to come into force and so it is the Appropriate Adult (AA) that assists; their role is to safeguard the rights, entitlements, and welfare of juveniles and vulnerable suspects (Code C, 2018, para, 1.7). However, despite their introduction into PACE, Code C, research has consistently documented the difficulties in implementing them when required (Bath & Dehaghani, 2020; Bradley, 2009; Medford et al., 2003; NAAN, 2015; Young et al., 2013). Indeed, the work of Farrugia (2021) highlights how even when vulnerability is identified, implementing the AA is driven by factors such as severity of mental health condition or disorder and comprehension difficulties. This is in line with other recent research and has implications for the use of the AA; even when vulnerability is identified, utilising the appropriate safeguards remains a subjective decision (Dehaghani, 2019; McKinnon & Finch, 2018).

Such implications are also important when considering liaison and diversion (L&D) services. Quite often, individuals with mental health conditions and disorders only access the relevant care services when they have been arrested, and so it is imperative that vulnerability is identified appropriately, and relevant safeguards and processes are implemented. L&D services are a relatively new concept and attempt to divert vulnerable individuals away from the CJS and into the appropriate health and social care services (College of Policing, 2016). Although significant national funding has been sought (Kane et al., 2020), the limited evidence base remains mixed for the success of L&D services (Disley et al., 2021; Kane et al., 2018, 2020; Scott et al., 2013), and as such it appears there remains more work to do in identifying the vulnerable suspect and implementing the necessary safeguards and, where appropriate, diverting such vulnerable individuals away from the CJS.

Safeguards in the Criminal Justice System: The Appropriate Adult

Vulnerable suspects, especially those with mental health conditions and disorders, have reported not knowing what to say or do when being interviewed by the police (Hyun et al., 2014), and are at a heightened risk of providing false confessions (Gudjonsson, 2018). As such, the AA plays a vital role in assisting vulnerable suspects during the interview process (Heide & Chan, 2016). Little research has explored the AA role, although of the limited research base, most seems to suggest that the AA remains passive and unengaged (Evans, 1993; Pierpoint, 2001). The work of Farrugia and Gabbert (2019a) explored this further; they too reported that AAs failed to intervene when reasonably expected and that these missed opportunities were significantly more common than the AA making an intervention. They also found that when AAs were intervening, it was more likely to be an appropriate intervention than an inappropriate one. Together this means that although AAs contributions are appropriate in nature, they still do not appear to be fulfilling their role as outlined by current legislative practice (PACE, 1984). There are now a handful of studies that suggest the passivity of the AA (Evans, 1993; Pierpoint, 2001).

These findings raise issues that are important to address; especially so given the recent estimates that over a third of suspects in police custody have mental health conditions or disorders (Leese & Russell, 2017). It is well documented that such vulnerable suspects are at a heightened risk of providing inaccurate and unreliable information and are highly suggestible (Gudjonsson, 2018; Kassin & Gudjonsson, 2004; Littlechild, 2001; NAAN, 2015; Redlich, 2004). Such inherent difficulties are likely to be exacerbated if the AA is not assisting them when required.

Despite the AA being described as passive in their role, very little research has explored how the AA *actually* understands and experiences their role when enacting it. The AA role has been described as a confusing and demanding one (Bartlett & Sandland, 2003; Cummins, 2011), with some suggestions that it may be socially constructed, and thus perceived in different ways dependent on the individual involved in the CJS (Pierpoint, 2006). Such confusion extends to the AA themselves, with some research documenting that many AAs may not fully understand their role, may be compliant with or disempowered by the police, and thus not make the appropriate interventions (Nemitz & Bean, 2001). This was explored further in the work of Farrugia (submitted). Her findings suggest that the role of the AA is not well understood by the AA themselves and other professionals working in the CJS. Furthermore, AAs reported some positive but largely negative experiences when enacting their role relating to conflicts with police officers and solicitors. AAs highlighted the impact that this would have on further interventions with some suggesting that it has reduced the likelihood of them intervening. Drawing on Social Identity Theory (Tajfel & Turner, 1979), Farrugia (submitted) explained that individuals will make significant concessions, such as avoiding conflicts, to remain in their in-group and so AAs may become passive to avoid further conflict with those that they are working with. Thus, the work of Farrugia (submitted) provides some insight into the passivity of the AA that has been documented previously.

This raises a number of issues; if AAs are remaining passive to avoid further conflict, then this heightens the risk of false confessions and miscarriages of justice given the vulnerabilities that those with mental health conditions and disorders may present with. In addition, if the AA is deemed to be passive, they may not be valued and thus professionals may be less inclined to engage with them. Ultimately, high numbers of vulnerable suspects will continue to enter custody and so it is essential that they have the necessary safeguards who are able to enact their role to their full potential.

The Vulnerable Suspect and the Investigative Interview

Individuals with mental health conditions and disorders do not respond well to traditional methods of policing (Gudjonsson, 2018) and their needs are not well understood (Baksheev et al., 2010). Interviewing such vulnerable suspects is not an easy task (Herrington & Roberts, 2012; L. Oxburgh et al., 2016) but those involved in this stage need to have an understanding of how they are likely to engage and communicate (Powell, 2002). The presentation of a vulnerable suspect may be dependent upon their specific mental health condition or disorder. For example, individuals with mood disorders have been found to have specific deficits in control of attention, recall, and episodic memory (Beck, 1976, 1987; Beevers & Carver, 2003; Beevers et al., 2009; Blaney, 1986; Lemogne et al., 2006; Mathews & MacLeod, 2005; Rude et al., 2002). This is also the case in those that have anxiety (Airaksinen et al., 2005); these individuals tend to present with an attentional bias towards negative stimuli which subsequently interferes with performance in other attentional tasks (Bar-Haim et al., 2007; Cisler & Koster, 2010; Macleod & Mathews, 2012). Individuals with schizophrenia also tend to have cognitive impairments relating to attention, processing speed and memory (Ragland et al., 2009). In addition to specific impairments, those with mental health conditions and disorders may also exhibit general vulnerabilities such as an overgeneral memory (Williams, 1996; Williams et al., 2007) and heightened levels of suggestibility, compliance, and acquiescence (Gudjonsson, 2010, 2018).

This has implications for the investigative interview and the free recall element. The impairments found in those with depression could result in opportunities for rumination, and the open question used to initiate the free recall, may not provide enough structured instructions to control the attention (Hertel, 1998; Hertel & Rude, 1991). In individuals with anxiety, seeking the free recall and thus drawing on the episodic memory can be difficult in that processing efficiency theory (Eysenck & Calvo, 1992) suggests that anxious worry reduces the capacity of memory and increases the effort needed to perform this task. The ability to retain information and use it to respond to a question is also dependent upon cognitive load (Vytal et al., 2012, 2013). For those that have schizophrenia, tasks that involve high cognitive demand are found to exacerbate impairments in episodic memory (Guo et al., 2019) – that is, there is likely to be reduced accuracy and the need for longer response time in recall (Fusar-Poli et al., 2012; Jonides et al., 2008; van Merrienboer & Sweller, 2010; White et al., 2010). As such, vulnerable suspects may find it difficult to recall specific events and in the correct order, may demonstrate difficulties in concentrating and attending to questions asked of them (Kingdon & Turkington, 2005), thus leading to errors or a reduction in performance – that is, their recall during the interview (Engle & Kane, 2004; Strayer & Drews, 2007). Subsequently, vulnerable suspects may falsely implicate themselves due to the impairments in their episodic and working memory and the impact of the interview – a cognitively demanding task.

Little research has focused specifically on this in the investigative interview with suspects that have mental health conditions or disorders. However, within the vulnerable witness literature, there appears to be an emerging branch of research that suggests that open questions and the free recall technique is not appropriate for all vulnerable groups (Bowles & Sharman, 2014; Perlman et al., 1994; Ternes & Yuille, 2008). The work of Farrugia and Gabbert (2019b) also highlights this; their results suggested that open questions may not be entirely suitable for suspects with mental health conditions or disorders in terms of the cognitive abilities and amount of information elicited. This suggests that best practice may not be best practice for this vulnerable group. Interestingly, their findings also corroborate previous studies that show that significantly more inappropriate questions are still used in suspect interviews than appropriate questions (Myklebust & Alison, 2000; Snook & Keating, 2011; Wright & Alison, 2004). Thus, despite the implementation of the PEACE model of interviewing, police officers still appear to be utilising questions that are currently categorised in the psychological literature as 'inappropriate,' and the vulnerable suspects' needs are not being entirely met.

A Paradigm Shift?

Research investigating how suspects with mental health conditions and disorders cope during the investigative interview is scarce, despite numerous concerns being raised (Carey, 2001; Dew & Badger, 1999; L. Oxburgh et al., 2016; Psarra et al., 2008; Wells & Schafer, 2006). This is problematic, especially when one considers the developments in interview techniques for vulnerable witnesses. For example, the Cognitive Interview (CI; Fisher & Geiselman, 1992), originally developed for use with witnesses has undergone many adaptations – the mental reinstatement of context has been replaced with the sketch-reinstatement of context for use with witnesses with an Autism Spectrum Condition (ASC, Mattison et al., 2015, 2018). Furthermore, the Self-Administered Interview (SAI; Gabbert et al., 2009), another version of the CI, has been developed to assist in obtaining an account immediately or as soon as possible after the witnessed event, although research regarding its efficiency with vulnerable populations is still very much in its infancy. More recently, the Witness-Aimed First Account (WAFA; Maras et al., 2020) has been designed as an interview technique for witnesses that have an ASC – this method allows the witness to provide their own specific prompts as part of their free recall which are then explored in turn. Early research suggests positive findings (Maras et al., 2020).

Despite the increasing number of interview techniques being designed to assist vulnerable witnesses, there appears to be a dearth of work that has focused specifically on the vulnerable suspect, particularly those with mental health conditions and disorders. This is concerning given the inherent risk vulnerable suspects are at during their time in the CJS. The work of Farrugia and Gabbert (2020) is one of the first to explore a modified interview style during interviews with participants (experimental suspects) that had mental health conditions and disorders. Their findings found a higher amount of information and more accurate information was elicited in response to the modified interview, that used more specific and closed questions, rather than the best practice interview that utilised open questions. Furthermore, less confusion was demonstrated by the vulnerable participants in the modified interview. This indicates that the use of specific questions may provide scaffolding to individuals with mental health conditions or disorders and thus reduce the impact on their cognition that a free recall, open question interview can otherwise impose (White et al., 2009). Such findings continue to challenge whether best practice really is best practice for such vulnerable suspects and has implications for the investigative interview; whilst it is not being suggested that vulnerable suspects should be interviewed without using open questions, it must be considered that an alternative question strategy may be better suited to the needs of suspects with mental health conditions and disorders.

Recommendations for Future Research and Final Conclusions

The replication of psychological research is vital in ensuring the validity and reliability of research findings (Cohen, 1994; Roediger, 2012). This is never more important when considering the applied nature of research regarding the investigative interview with the vulnerable suspect and the subsequent impact it can have on the rest of the investigation; policy change or development must be underpinned by strong, robust research findings that ensure confidence. The subject area concerning the interviewing of suspects with mental health conditions and disorders is relatively under-researched and the research studies that have been conducted recently are relatively new to the field or are based on dated research studies that have not been replicated since. The research presented in this monograph adds to the limited literature and provides an interesting insight into an emerging pool of research that suggests best practice questioning strategies may not be suitable for vulnerable suspects. However, replication is necessary before any change to policy or practice is advocated for. This is certainly an area that warrants further attention by academics, practitioners, and policymakers alike.

How vulnerable individuals are identified, perceived, and dealt with in the CJS by the various professionals they may encounter requires further work, simply because this has an impact on the way that they are treated and their subsequent outcomes in the CJS. There still exists some uncertainty as to what constitutes a mental health condition or disorder and the impact this can have on the vulnerable suspect. This is true also of the safeguards that vulnerable suspects are entitled to. For example, the role of the AA; whilst recent work provides some insight into the AAs own experience, more work is necessary to explore further how this may impact on AAs assisting vulnerable suspects. Insight from the vulnerable suspect themselves would be useful to understand how they perceive this crucial safeguard, as well as professionals working alongside the AA. Findings suggest that should an AA experience conflict in their role, this impacts upon their interventions and so their assistance with the vulnerable suspect may become limited (Farrugia, submitted). Thus, the vulnerable suspect is not receiving the safeguard they need.

Interviewing vulnerable suspects is a difficult task and one that may be exacerbated by the specific cognitive difficulties that suspects with mental health conditions and disorders may present with. Findings from analysing real-life suspect interviews suggest that these vulnerable suspects do not respond well to best practice questioning methods (Farrugia & Gabbert, 2019b). This was also reported from experimental work that tested an alternative interview model – one of the most important findings is that different vulnerable suspect groups may require different interviewing methods. This is particularly compelling when added to earlier findings that show that adults with an intellectual disability report fewer correct details than those without an intellectual disability when asked open questions that invite a free narrative response (Bowles & Sharman, 2014; Perlman et al., 1994; Ternes & Yuille, 2008). Further work needs to examine this, particularly as the work of Farrugia and Gabbert (2019b) focused on mental health conditions and disorders as a whole, and not specific individual conditions. Whilst there exist many commonalities across all mental health conditions and disorders (for example, heightened levels of suggestibility), it must be acknowledged that there are a large amount of mental health conditions and disorders, and each represents its own different vulnerabilities. Further work should examine suspects with specific groups of mental health conditions and disorders to gain a further understanding of their impact upon the investigative interview process.

There has been a great deal of work completed in recent decades which has resulted in the move away from an interrogatory, confession-seeking ethos to a systematic model, underpinned by psychological research, that emphasises the obtaining of reliable and accurate information (see Williamson, 2006). However, the interviewing of suspects with mental health conditions and disorders has not received much psychological attention. As such, a substantial amount of further work is required. Further work will lead to an understanding of the needs of this type of vulnerable suspect which will subsequently ensure that their vulnerabilities are not exacerbated during the investigative interview. Currently, suspects with mental health problems remains one of the largest challenges within the criminal justice system and is one that the interviewing officer continuously faces; is best practice *really* best practice for this vulnerable group?

References

Abramson, M. (1972). The criminalisation of mentally disordered behaviour: A possible side effect of a new mental health law. *Hospital and Community Psychiatry, 23*, 101–105.

Airaksinen, E., Larsson, M., & Forsell, Y. (2005). Neuropsychological functions in anxiety disorders in population-based samples: Evidence of episodic memory dysfunction. *Journal of Psychiatric Research, 39*, 207–214.

Anderson, R. (1977). The notion of schemata and the educational enterprise: General discussion of the conference. In R. Anderson, R. Spiro, & W. Montague (Eds.), *Schooling and the acquisition of knowledge* (pp. 415–432). Hillsdale: Erlbaum.

Baksheev, G., Ogloff, J., & Thomas, S. (2012). Identification of mental illness in police cells: A comparison of police processes, the brief jail mental health screen and the jail screening assessment tool. *Psychology, Crime and Law, 18*, 529–542.

Baksheev, G., Thomas, S., & Ogloff, J. (2010). Psychiatric disorders and unmet needs in Australian police cells. *Australian and New Zealand Journal of Psychiatry, 44*, 1043–1051.Bar-Haim, Y., Lamy, D., Pergamin, L., Bakermans-Kranenburg, M., & van Ijzendoorn, M. (2007). Threat-related attentional bias in anxious and nonanxious individuals: A meta-analytic study. *Psychological Bulletin, 133*, 1–24.

Bartlett, P. & Sandland, R. (2003). *Mental health law policy and practice.* Oxford: Oxford University Press.

Bath, C. & Dehaghani, R. (2020). *There to help 3. The identification of vulnerable adult suspects and application of the appropriate adult safeguard in police investigations in 2018/19.* London: National Appropriate Adult Network.

Bather, P., Fitzpatrick, R., & Rutherford, M. (2008). *Briefing 36: Police and mental health.* London: Sainsbury Centre for Mental Health.

Beck, A. (1976). *Cognitive therapy and the emotional disorders.* Oxford: International Universities Press.

Beck, A. (1987). Cognitive models of depression. *Journal of Cognitive Psychotherapy, 1*, 5–37.

Beevers, C. & Carver, C. (2003). Attentional bias and mood persistence as prospective predictors of dysphoria. *Cognitive Therapy and Research, 27*, 619–637.

Beevers, C., Wells, T., Ellis, A., & McGeary, J. (2009). Association of the serotonin transporter gene promotor region (5-HTTLPR) polymorphism with biased attention for emotional stimuli. *Journal of Abnormal Psychology, 118*(3), 670–681.

Blaney, P. (1986). Affect and memory: A review. *Psychological Bulletin, 99*, 229–246.

Bowles, P. & Sharman, S. (2014). A review of the impact of different types of leading interview questions on child and adult witnesses with intellectual disabilities. *Psychiatry, Psychology and Law, 21*(2), 205–217.

Bradley, K. (2009). *The Bradley Report: Lord Bradley's review of people with mental health problems or learning disabilities in the criminal justice system.* London: Department of Health.

Bull, R. (2010). The investigative interviewing of children and other vulnerable witnesses: Psychological research and working/professional practice. *Legal and Criminological Psychology, 15,* 5–23.

Cant, R. & Standen, P. (2007). What professionals think about offenders with learning disabilities in the criminal justice system. *British Journal of Learning Disabilities, 35,* 174–180.

Carey, S. (2001). Police officers' knowledge of, and attitudes to mental illness in Southwest Scotland. *Scottish Medical Journal, 46,* 41–42.

Case, B., Steadman, H., Dupis, S., & Morris, L. (2009). Who succeeds in jail diversion programs? A multi-site study. *Behavioural Sciences and Law, 27*(5), 661–674.

Cisler, J. & Koster, E. (2010). Mechanisms of attentional biases towards threat in the anxiety disorders: An integrative review. *Clinical Psychology Review, 30*(2), 203–216.

Clarke, C. & Milne, R. (2001). *National evaluation of the PEACE investigative interviewing course. Police Research Award Scheme, Report No. PRAS/149.* Institute of Criminal Justice Studies, Portsmouth.

Cohen, J. (1994). The earth is round (p < .05). *American Psychologist, 49,* 997–1003.

College of Policing. (2014). *National Decision Model.* www.app.college.police. uk/app-content/national-decision-model/the-national decision-model/

College of Policing. (2016). *Mental health and the criminal justice system.* www. app.college.police.uk/app-content/mental-health/crime-and-criminal justice/

College of Policing. (2017). *Detention and custody. Risk assessment.* www.app. college.police.uk/app-content/detention-and-custody-2/risk   assessment/ #content-of-risk-assessments

College of Policing. (2018). *Authorised professional practice.* www.app.college. police.uk/

Cummins, I. (2011). 'The other side of silence': The role of the appropriate adult post Bradley. *Ethics and Social Welfare, 5*(3), 306–312.

Daff, E. & Thomas, S. (2014). Bipolar disorder and criminal offending: A data linkage study. *Social Psychiatry and Psychiatric Epidemiology, 49,* 1985–1991.

Dehaghani, R. (2019). *Vulnerability in police custody. Police decision-making and the appropriate adult safeguard.* London: Routledge.

Dew, K. & Badger, S. (1999). Police perceptions of the mental health services and the mentally ill. *New Zealand Medical Journal, 112,* 36–38.

Disley, E., Gkousis, E., Hulme, S., Morley, K., Pollard, J., Saunders, C., Sussex, J., & Sutherland, A. (2021). *Outcome evaluation of the national model for liaison and diversion.* Cambridge: RAND.

Douglas, K., Vincent, G., & Edens, J. (2006). Risk of criminal recidivism: the role of psychopathy. In C. Patrick (Ed.), *Handbook of psychopathy* (pp. 533–554). New York: Guildford Press.

Drizin, S. & Leo, R. (2004). The problem of false confessions in the post-DNA world. *North Carolina Law Review, 82*, 891–1007.

Engle, R. & Kane, M. (2004). Executive attention, working memory capacity, and a two-factor theory of cognitive control. *Psychology of Learning and Motivation, 44*, 145–200.

Evans, R. (1993). *The conduct of police interviews with young people*. Royal Commission on Criminal Justice Research Study No.8. London: HMSO.

Eysenck, M. & Calvo, M. (1992). Anxiety and performance: The processing efficiency theory. *Cognitive and Emotion, 6*, 409–434.

Farrugia, L. (2021). Identifying vulnerability in police custody: Making sense of information provided to custody officers. *Journal of Forensic and Legal Medicine, 80*, 102169.

Farrugia, L. (submitted). The 'professional' appropriate adult: Their perspective. *Submitted to Policing.*

Farrugia, L. & Gabbert, F. (2019a). The appropriate adult: What they do and what they should do in police interviews with mentally disordered suspects. *Criminal Behaviour and Mental Health, 29*(3), 134–141.

Farrugia, L. & Gabbert, F. (2019b). Vulnerable suspects in police interviews: Exploring current practice in England and Wales. *Journal of Investigative Psychology and Offender Profiling, 17*(1), 17–30.

Farrugia, L. & Gabbert, F. (2020). Forensic interviewing of mentally disordered suspects: the impact of interview style on investigation outcomes. *Current Psychology*, 1–9. DOI: https://doi.org/10.1007/s12144-020-00747-8

Fazel, S. & Seewald, K. (2012). Severe mental illness in 33,588 prisoners worldwide: Systematic review and meta-regression analysis. *The British Journal of Psychiatry, 200*, 364–373.

Fisher, H. (1977). *Report of an inquiry by the Hon. Sir Henry Fisher into the circumstances leading to the trial of three persons on charges arising out of the death of Maxwell Confait and the fire at 27 Doggett Road, London, SE6.* London: HMSO.

Fisher, R. & Geiselman, R. (1992). *Memory-enhancing techniques for investigative interviewing: The cognitive interview.* Springfield, IL: Charles C. Thomas.

Fisher, W., Silver, E., & Wolff, N. (2006). Beyond criminalisation: Toward a criminologically informed framework for mental health policy and services research. *Administration and Policy in Mental Health and Mental Health Services Research, 33*(5), 544–557.

Fusar-Poli, P., Deste, G., Smieskova, R., Barlati, S., Yung, A., & Howes, O. (2012). Cognitive functioning in prodromal psychosis: A meta-analysis. *Archives of General Psychiatry, 69*(6), 562–571.

Gabbert, F., Hope, L., & Fisher, R. (2009). Protecting eyewitness evidence: Examining the efficacy of a self-administered interview tool. *Law and Human Behaviour, 33*, 298–307.

Griffiths, A. & Milne, R. (2006). Will it all end in tiers? Police interviews with suspects in Britain. In T. Williamson (Ed.), *Investigative interviewing: Rights, research, regulation* (pp. 167–189). Cullompton: Willan.

Gudjonsson, G. (2006). The psychological vulnerabilities of witnesses and the risk of false accusations and false confessions. In A. Heaton-Armstrong, E. Shepherd, G. Gudjonsson, & D. Wolchover (Eds.), *Witness testimony. Psychological, investigative and evidential perspectives* (pp. 61–75). Oxford: Oxford University Press.

Gudjonsson, G. (2010). Psychological vulnerabilities during police interviews: Why are they important? *Legal and Criminological Psychology, 15*(2), 161–175.

Gudjonsson, G. (2018). *The psychology of false confessions: Forty years of science and practice.* West Sussex: Wiley.

Guo, J., Ragland, R., & Carter, C. (2019). Memory and cognition in schizophrenia. *Molecular Psychiatry, 24*(5), 633–642.

Heide, S. & Chan, T. (2016). Deaths in police custody. *Journal of Forensic and Legal Medicine, 57,* 109–114.

Herrington, V. & Roberts, K. (2012). Addressing psychological vulnerability in the police suspect interview. *Policing, 6,* 1–10.

Hertel, P. (1998). Relation between rumination and impaired memory in dysphoric moods. *Journal of Abnormal Psychology, 107,* 166–172.

Hertel, P. & Rude, S. (1991). Depressive deficits in memory. Focusing attention improves subsequent recall. *Journal of Experimental Psychology: General, 120,* 301–309.

Home Office. (1981). *Royal Commission on Criminal Procedure.* London: HMSO

Home Office. (1984). *Police and Criminal Evidence Act (1984) and Codes of Practice (2018).* London: Home Office.

Hyun, E., Hahn, L., & McConnell, D. (2014). Experiences of people with learning disabilities in the Criminal Justice System. *British Journal of Learning Disabilities, 42,* 308–314.

Inbau, F., Reid, J., Buckley, J., & Jayne, B. (2013). *Criminal interrogation and confessions.* Burlington, MA: Jones & Bartlett Learning.

Jonides, J., Lewis, R., Nee, D., Lustig, C., Berman, M., & Moore, K. (2008). The mind and brain of short-term memory. *Annual Review of Psychology, 59,* 193–224.

Junginger, J., Claypoole, C., Ranilo, I., & Crisanti, A. (2006). Effects of serious mental illness and substance abuse on criminal offences. *Psychiatric Services, 57*(6), 879–882.

Kane, E., Evans, E., Mitsch, J., & Jilani, T. (2020). Are liaison and diversion interventions in policing delivering the planned impact: A longitudinal evaluation in two constabularies? *Criminal Behaviour and Mental Health, 30,* 256–267.

Kane, E., Evans, E., & Shokraneh, F. (2018). Effectiveness of current policing-related mental health interventions: A systematic review. *Criminal Behaviour and Mental Health, 28*(2), 108–119.

Kassin, S. (2005). On the psychology of confessions: Does innocence put innocents at risk? *American Psychologist, 60,* 215–228.

Kassin, S. (2012). Why confessions trump innocence. *American Psychologist*, *67*, 431–445.

Kassin, S. & Gudjonsson, G. (2004). The psychology of confessions: A review of the literature and issues. *Psychological Science in the Public Interest*, *5*, 33–67.

Kassin, S. & Wrightsman, L. (1985). Confession evidence. In S. Kassin & L. Wrightsman (Eds.), *The psychology of evidence and trial procedure* (pp.67–94). London: Sage

Kingdon, D. & Turkington, D. (2005). *Cognitive therapy for schizophrenia.* New York: Guildford.

Leese, M. & Russell, S. (2017). Mental health, vulnerability and risk in police custody. *Journal of Adult Protection*, *19*(5), 274–283.

Lemogne, C., Piolino, P., Friszer, S., Claret, A., Girault, N., Jouvent, R., Allilaire, J., & Fossati, P. (2006). Episodic autobiographical memory in depression: specificity, autonetic consciousness, and self-perspective. *Consciousness and Cognition*, *15*, 258–268.

Link, B., Phelan, J., Bresnahan, M., Stueve, A., & Pescosolido, B. (1999). Public perceptions of mental illness: Labels, causes, dangerousness, and social distance. *American Journal of Public Health, 89*, 1328–1333.

Littlechild, B. (2001). *Appropriate Adults and Appropriate Adult schemes: Service user, provider and police perspectives.* Birmingham: Venture Press.

Macleod, C. & Mathews, A. (2012). Cognitive bias modification approaches to anxiety. *Annual Review of Clinical Psychology*, *8*, 189–217.

Maras, K., Dando, C., Stephenson, H., Lambrechts, A., Anns, S., & Gaigg, S. (2020). The witness-aimed first account (WAFA): A new technique for interviewing autistic witnesses and victims. *Autism*, *24*(6), 1449–1467.

Mathews, A. & MacLeod, C. (2005). Cognitive vulnerability to emotional disorders. *Annual Review of Clinical Psychology, 1*, 167–195.

Mattison, M., Dando, C., & Ormerod, T. (2015). Sketching to remember: Episodic free recall task support fort child witnesses and victims with autism spectrum disorder. *Journal of Autism and Developmental Disorders*, *45*, 1751–1765.

Mattison, M., Dando, C., & Ormerod, T. (2018). Drawing the answers: Sketching to support free and probed recall by child witnesses and victims with autism spectrum disorder. *Autism*, *22*(2), 181–194.

McKinnon, I. & Finch, T. (2018). Contextualising health screening risk assessments in police custody suites – qualitative evaluation from the HELP-PC study in London, UK. *BMC Public Health*, *18*, 393–406.

McKinnon, I. & Grubin, D. (2010). Health screening in police custody. *Journal of Forensic and Legal Medicine*, *17*, 209–212.

McKinnon, I. & Grubin, D. (2013). Health screening of people in police custody evaluation of current police screening procedures in London, UK. *European Journal of Public Health*, *23*(3), 399–405.

McKinnon, I. & Grubin, D. (2014). Evidence-based risk assessment screening in police custody: The HELP-PC study in London, UK. *Policing, 8*(2), 174–182.

Medford, S., Gudjonsson, G., & Pearse, J. (2003). The efficacy of the appropriate adult safeguard during police interviewing. *Legal and Criminological Psychology, 8*(2), 253–266.

Ministry of Justice. (2011). *Achieving best evidence in criminal proceedings: Guidance on interviewing victims and witnesses and using special measures.* London: HMSO.

Murray, J., Heyman, I., Wooff, A., Dougall, N., Aston, L., & Enang, I. (2018). *Law enforcement and public health: Setting the agenda for Scotland.* Dundee: Scottish Institute for Policing Research Annual Review.

Myklebust, T. (2009). *Analysis of field investigative interviews of children conducted by specially trained police investigators.* Unpublished PhD thesis. University of Oslo.

Myklebust, T. & Alison, L. (2000). The current state of police interviews with children in Norway: How discrepant are they from models based on current issues in memory and communication? *Psychology, Crime and Law, 6,* 331–351.

National Appropriate Adult Network. (2015). *There to help: Ensuring provision of appropriate adults for mentally vulnerable adults detained or interviewed by police.* www.appropriateadult.org.uk/images/pdf/2015_theretohelpcomplete.pdf

Nemitz, T. & Bean, P. (2001). Protecting the rights of the MD in police stations: The use of the Appropriate Adult in England and Wales. *International Journal of Law and Psychiatry, 24,* 595–605.

Neumann, C. & Hare, R. (2008). Psychopathic traits in a large community sample: Links to violence, alcohol use, and intelligence. *Journal of Consulting and Clinical Psychology, 76,* 893–899.

Noga, L., Walsh, E., Shaw, J., & Senior, J. (2015). The development of a mental health screening tool and referral pathway for police custody. *The European Journal of Public Health, 25*(2), 237–242.

Oxburgh, L., Gabbert, F., Milne, R., & Cherryman, J. (2016). Police officers' perceptions and experiences with MD suspects. *International Journal of Law and Psychiatry, 49,* 138–146.

Oxburgh, G., Myklebust, T., & Grant, T. (2010a). The question of question types in police interviews: A review of the literature from a psychological and linguistic perspective. *International Journal of Speech, Language and the Law, 17,* 45–66.

Oxburgh, G., Ost, J., & Cherryman, J. (2010b). Police interviews with suspected child sex offenders: Does use of empathy and question type influence the amount of investigation relevant information obtained? *Psychology, Crime and Law, 18*(3), 1–15.

Perlman, N., Ericson, K., Esses, V., & Isaacs, B. (1994). The developmentally handicapped witness: Competency as a function of question format. *Law and Human Behaviour, 18,* 171–187.

Peterson, J., Skeem, J., Hart, E., Vidal, S., & Keith, F. (2010). Analysing offence patterns as a function of mental illness to test the criminalisation hypothesis. *Psychiatric Services, 61*(12), 1217–1222.

Phillips, E., Oxburgh, G., & Myklebust, T. (2011). Investigative interviews with victims of child sexual abuse: The relationship between question and investigation relevant information. *Journal of Police and Criminal Psychology, 27*, 45–54.

Pierpoint, H. (2001). The performance of volunteer appropriate adults: A survey of call outs. *Howard Journal of Criminal Justice, 40*(3), 255–271.

Pierpoint, H. (2006). Reconstructing the role of the Appropriate Adult in England and Wales. *Criminology and Criminal Justice, 6*, 219–237.

Powell, M. (2002). Specialist training in investigative and evidential interviewing: Is it having any effect on the behaviour of professionals in the field? *Psychiatry, Psychology and Law, 9*, 44–55.

Price, C. & Caplan, J. (1977). *The Confait confessions.* London: Boyars.

Psarra, V., Sestrini, M., Santa, Z., Petsas, D., Gerontas, A., Garnetas, C., & Kontis, K. (2008). Greek police officers' attitudes towards the mentally ill. *International Journal of Law and Psychiatry, 31*, 77–85.

Ragland, J., Laird, A., Ranganath, C., Blumenfeld, R., Gonzales, S., & Glahn, D. (2009). Prefrontal activation deficits during episodic memory in schizophrenia. *American Journal of Psychiatry, 166*(8), 863–874.

Redlich, A. (2004). Mental illness, police interrogations, and the potential for false confession. *Law and Psychiatry, 55*, 19–21.

Roediger, H. (2012). Psychology's woes and a partial cure: The value of replication. *APS Observer, 25*, 27–29.

Rude, S., Wenzlaff, R., Gibbs, B., Vane, J., & Whitney, T. (2002). Negative processing biases predict subsequent depressive symptoms. *Cognition and Emotion, 16*, 423–440.

Scheff, T. (1966). Users and non-users of a student psychiatric clinic. *Journal of Health and Human Behaviour, 7*, 114–121.

Scheff, T. (1984). *Being mentally ill.* Piscataway: Aldine Transaction.

Scott, D., McGilloway, S., Dempster, M., Browne, F., & Donnelly, M. (2013). Effectiveness of criminal justice liaison and diversion services for offenders with mental disorders: A review. *Psychiatric Services, 64*(9), 843–849.

Snook, B. & Keating, K. (2011). A field study of adult witness interviewing practices in a Canadian police organisation. *Legal and Criminological Psychology, 16*(1), 160–172.

Snook, B., Luther, K., Quinlan, H., & Milne, R. (2012). Let 'em talk! A field study of police questioning practices of suspects and accused persons. *Criminal Justice and Behaviour, 39*(10), 1328–1339.

Soukara, S., Bull, R., Vrij, A., Turner, M., & Cherryman, J. (2009). What really happens in police interviews of suspects? Tactics and confessions. *Psychology, Crime and Law, 15*, 493–506.

Strayer, D. & Drews, F. (2007). Cell-phone-induced driver distraction. *Current Directions in Psychological Science, 16*(3), 128–131.

Tajfel, H. & Turner, J. (1979). An integrative theory of intergroup conflict. In G. Austin, & S. Worchel (Eds.), *The social psychology of intergroup relations* (pp. 33–47). Monterey, CA: Brooks-Cole.

Ternes, M. & Yuille, J. (2008). Eyewitness memory and eyewitness identification performance in adults with intellectual disabilities. *Journal of Applied Research in Intellectual Disabilities, 21*, 519–531.

Tyler, T. & Blader, S. (2003). The group engagement model: Procedural justice social identity and cooperative behaviour. *Personality and Social Psychology Review, 7*, 349–361.

van Merrienboer, J. & Sweller, J. (2010). Cognitive load theory in health professional education: design principles and strategies. *Medical Education, 44*(1), 85–93.

Vytal, K., Cornwell, B., Arkin, N., & Grillon, C. (2012). Describing the interplay between anxiety and cognition: From impaired performance under low cognitive load to reduced anxiety under high load. *Psychophysiology, 49*, 842–852.

Vytal, K., Cornwell, B., Arkin, N., Letkiewicz, A., Grillon, C. (2013). The complex interaction between anxiety and cognition: Insight from spatial and verbal working memory. *Frontiers in Human Neuroscience, 7*, 93.

Walsh, D. & Bull, R. (2010). What really is effective in interviews with suspects? A study comparing interview skills against interviewing outcomes. *Legal and Criminological Psychology, 15*, 305–321.

Walsh, D. & Milne, R. (2008). Keeping the PEACE? A study of investigative interviewing practices in the public sector. *Legal and Criminological Psychology, 13*, 39–57.

Wells, W. & Schafer, J. (2006). Officer perceptions of police responses to persons with mental illness. *Policing: An International Journal of Police Strategies and Management, 29*, 578–601.

White, S., Burgess, P., & Hill, E. (2009). Impairments on "open-ended" executive function tests in autism. *Autism Research, 2*(3), 138–147.

White, T., Schmidt, M., & Karatekin, C. (2010). Verbal and visuospatial working memory development and deficits in children and adolescents with schizophrenia. *Early Intervention in Psychiatry, 4*(4), 305–313.

Williams, J. (1996). Depression and the specificity of autobiographical memory. In D. Rubin (Ed), *Remembering our past: Studies in autobiographical memory* (pp. 244–267). London: Cambridge University Press.

Williams, J., Barnhofer, T., Crane, C., Herman, D., & Raes, F. (2007). Autobiographical memory specificity and emotional disorder. *Psychological Bulletin, 133*, 122–148.

Williamson, T. (2006). *Investigative interviewing: Rights, research, regulation.* Devon: Willan.

Wright, A. & Alison, L. (2004). Questioning sequences in Canadian police interviews: Constructing and confirming the course of events? *Psychology, Crime and Law, 10*, 137–154.

Wright, R. & Powell, M. (2006). Investigative interviewers' perceptions of their difficulty to adhere to open-ended questions with child witnesses. *International Journal of Police Science and Management, 8*, 316–325.

Young, S., Goodwin, E., Sedgwick, O., & Gudjonsson, G. (2013). The effectiveness of police custody assessments in identifying suspects with intellectual disabilities and attention deficit hyperactivity disorder. *BMC Medicine, 11,* 248–259.

Youth Justice and Criminal Evidence Act. (1999). London: HMSO.

Index

Abrahamson, M. 30, 131
Achieving Best Evidence in Criminal
   Proceedings 26, 28–9, 42, 131;
   see also Special Measures
acquiescence 25, 92–4, 96–7, 102–3,
   110, 118–19, 123, 135
ANCOVA 120, 122–3
anorexia 118
anxiety 72, 89–90, 93, 98, 102, 118,
   135
Appropriate Adult 26, 28, 39, 49,
   51–2, 57, 62–3, 68, 69–84, 98,
   132–4, 137–8
Association of Chief Police Officers
   (ACPO) 14–15
attention deficit hyperactivity
   disorder (ADHD) 93
Authorised Professional Practice
   (APP) 14–18, 26, 47, 49–50, 62,
   130, 132
autismspectrum condition 52, 94–5,
   112–15, 123, 125, 136

Beck's schema model 89
behaviour analysis interview *see* Reid
   Interrogation Technique
body dysmorphic disorder 118
borderline personality disorder 72, 118
Bowers activation theory 89
Bradley, K. 50, 52, 60, 62–3, 132
bulimia 118

change order *see* cognitive interview
change perspective *see* cognitive
   interview

Chambliss 1973 *see* labelling theory
chi square 55–7
Clarke & Milne 2001 *see* PEACE
   model
cognitive interview 9, 111–13, 123–4,
   136; *see also* report everything;
   sketch reinstatement of context
   112, 123–4, 136
compliance 25, 28, 92–3, 95–7, 102–3,
   110, 118–19, 123, 135; *see also*
   Gudjonsson Compliance Scale
Communicourt 59
confession 1–2, 17, 51, 129–30, 138
Conversation Management
   Approach 9
Coroners and Justice Act 2009 28,
   59, 62
criminalisation hypothesis 30–1,
   41–2, 131

deception 2, 11, 17
depression 52, 72, 87–9, 92, 102, 118,
   135
dissociative identity disorder 72, 98
DSM-5 89–90

encoding specificity principle *see*
   mental reinstatement of context
episodic memory 89–91, 94, 102–3,
   115, 134–5
Equality Act 2010 10
Evans, R. 51, 68–9, 74, 133

false confessions 4–5, 16–17, 25, 68,
   83, 93, 102, 129, 133–4

Farrugia, L. 14, 28, 52–7, 62, 69–84, 95–103, 115–25, 130, 132, 133, 135, 136, 138
Fisher, H. 6, 129
Fisher, R. 12, 111, 136
Fisher Inquiry *see* miscarriages of justice
free recall *see* investigative interviewing

grounded theory 34–5
Gudjonsson Compliance Scale 92, 93
Gudjonsson, G. 4–5, 16, 25, 28, 30, 50, 68, 87, 92, 94, 102, 110, 118, 129, 132–5

HM Government *see* Mental Health Crisis Care Concordat
Human Rights Act 10

Inbau, F. 1–3, 129
innocence project 4
intellectual disabilities 94, 138; *see also* learning disability/ difficulties
Intermediaries for Justice 59
intermediary 29, 58–60, 62–3, 132; *see also* Registered Intermediary
Interpretative Phenomenological Analysis 76–7
interrogation 1, 7, 11, 17, 129, 138; *see also* Reid Interrogation Technique
investigative interviewing 7, 10, 12, 17, 32–4, 37–8, 68, 83, 87–103, 110–24, 129–31, 133–8; *see also* PEACE model
investigation relevant information 95–8, 100–2, 116–21, 124–5

labelling theory 32, 41, 131
learning disability/difficulties 116–17
liaison and diversion 60–3, 132
liaison and diversion operating model *see* liaison and diversion
loglinear analysis 55, 57

Mann Whitney U Test 99–100
memory 87–92, 102, 110–14, 123–4, 134–5; *see also* episodic memory;

working memory 90–1, 102, 135; overgeneral memory 92, 103, 135
Mendez, J. 12, 17
Mental Health Act 28, 30
Mental Health Crisis Care Concordat 60
mental reinstatement of context 111, 112, 136
Ministry of Justice 2011 *see* Achieving Best Evidence in Criminal Proceedings
miscarriages of justice 4–7, 16–17, 83, 129, 134
modified interview model *see* Farrugia
mood disorders 87–9, 98, 134; *see also* depression; bipolar disorder 87–9, 118

National Decision Model 16–18, 26, 49, 130
National Institute of Child Health and Human Development Protocol 11
NHS England Liaison and Diversion Programme *see* liaison and diversion

obsessive-compulsive disorder 118
Oxburgh, L. 14, 24, 33–41, 52, 95, 130–1, 134, 136

paranoid personality disorder 118
PEACE model, 7–11, 16–17, 96–7, 99, 110–11, 117, 124, 129–30, 136
personality disorder 98; *see also* paranoid personality disorder
Police and Criminal Evidence Act 1984 and associated Codes of Practice 6–7, 11, 16–17, 26–30, 41–2, 47, 49, 51, 62–3, 68–71, 82–4, 129–30, 132–3
Police Experience Transitional Model 35, 40–1, 131
post-traumatic stress disorder 92–3, 118
procedural justice theory 131
processing efficiency theory 90, 135
Professionalising Criminal Investigation Programme (PIP) 14–15, 17–18, 33–4, 130
psychoses 72, 98, 118

question type 12–13, 17–18, 38,
    87–9, 92, 94–103, 110, 115–16,
    118–19, 122, 124–5, 130–1,
    135–8

rapport 9, 11, 37, 42
Registered Intermediary 58–9
Reid Interrogation Technique 1–3,
    17, 129
replication 137
report everything 111
risk assessment 47–50, 62–3
Royal Commission on Criminal
    Procedure *see* miscarriages of
    justice
R (AS) *v.* Great Yarmouth Youth
    Court [2011] EWHC 2059
    (Admin), para 6 59
R (OP) *v.* Secretary of State for
    Justice [2014] EWHC 1944
    (Admin), para 41 59

schema theory 32, 40–1, 131
schizophrenia 52, 72, 90–2, 98, 103,
    134–5
Self-Administered Interview 112–14,
    123–4, 136
social identity theory 82–4, 134
Special Measures 26, 29, 58–9, 131
Structured Interview Protocol 13
suggestibility 25, 28, 92–3, 95–7,
    102–3, 110, 118–19, 123, 133,
    135, 138; *see also* Gudjonsson
    Suggestibility Scale

task support hypothesis 112
Triangle 59

Witness-Aimed First Account
    114–15, 123, 125, 136

Youth Justice and Criminal Evidence
    Act 26, 28–9, 42, 58–9, 62, 131